ΠE TOMORROW

Compiled and edited by
## DREW HAYDEN TAYLOR

An unravelling of linear time—INDIGENOUS FUTURISMS seek not only to IMAGINE Indigenous LIFE years into the FUTURE, but to contest chronological colonial visions of time—a DECONSTRUCTION, an ENVISIONING, a SUMMONING—*Me Tomorrow* constellates knowledge and invites discursive becoming, TRANSFORMING the NOW so as to reveal what has been and WHAT IS TO COME.

# Tomorrow

Indigenous Views on the Future

Douglas & McIntyre

1 2 3 4 5 — 25 24 23 22 21

Douglas and McIntyre (2013) Ltd.
P.O. Box 219, Madeira Park, BC, VON 2H0
www.douglas-mcintyre.com

Front cover art by Jordanna George

Cover design by Anna Comfort O'Keeffe and Shed Simas / Onça Design
Typesetting by Shed Simas / Onça Design
Printed and bound in Canada
100% recycled paper content

Douglas and McIntyre acknowledges the support of the Canada Council for
the Arts, the Government of Canada, and the Province of British Columbia
through the BC Arts Council.

LIBRARY AND ARCHIVES CANADA CATALOGUING IN PUBLICATION
Title: Me tomorrow : Indigenous views on the future / compiled and
    edited by Drew Hayden Taylor.
Names: Taylor, Drew Hayden, 1962- editor.
Identifiers: Canadiana (print) 20210276037 | Canadiana (ebook)
    20210277106 | ISBN 9781771622943 (softcover) | ISBN
    9781771622950 (EPUB)
Subjects: LCSH: Indigenous peoples—Canada. | LCSH: Indigenous
    peoples—Canada—Social life and customs. | LCSH: Indigenous
    peoples—Canada—Social conditions. | LCSH: Future, The.
Classification: LCC E78.C2 M4 2021 | DDC 305.897/071—dc23

# Contents

# Introduction

THESE ARE CHANGING TIMES.

For the first time, robins are appearing in the Arctic. Indigenous languages, once on the verge of disappearing, are now being strengthened via apps on cell phones. There's even been an Indigenous astronaut.

Once thought of as the disappearing Indians, it's comforting to know we haven't quite disappeared. In fact, we are more visible and vibrant than ever. More interestingly, we have adapted to pretty much everything the dominant culture has thrown at us and, even better, persevered.

Welcome to the fourth in the *Me* series, a collection of books exploring various aspects of Indigenous life. In past volumes we've delved into the concepts of humour, sexuality and how our heritage inspires and encourages our art forms. That was the past; now we're going in the other direction.

*Me Tomorrow* is a foray into what the future might hold. Within these covers are essays by individuals who are talking loudly and proudly about our future. There's frequently this impression that Indigenous people are always looking backward, at what we are trying to get back or reclaim. This book turns that lens around. The contributors are looking at where we will be—or should be—in the near future. You, the reader, will get a sense of pride as you read the contents of this book, and possibly wonder where you might fit into that future.

Coming from the Four Directions, our Elders, academics, youth, artists, politicians et al. have something to say. Perspectives range from politics, to environment, to education, to so many more. Our world is a complex one and what's in this book is just the tip of the proverbial iceberg.

As the saying goes, you cannot know where you are going without understanding where you've been. So the people who have envisioned the future have filtered their understanding through journeys their Ancestors have already made. That's what makes this book so cool.

With that said, I hope you will find these experiences, these stories, these hopes, as fascinating as I have. I am so honoured to have gathered these knowledgeable people together.

Tomorrow starts today.

DREW HAYDEN TAYLOR
Curve Lake First Nation
March 2021

# About the Cover Art

"**M**OTHERBOARD" IS A NOD TO HOW INDIGENOUS people's relationship to the land and water is not merely a historical notion but a connection that persists in the present and will be sustained far into the future. This connection, much like Indigenous Peoples themselves, has survived and adapted through centuries of colonialism, industrialization and countless other forms of change. This piece represents that adaptation. It is a look at the blending of traditional motifs with contemporary aesthetics, as well as adding an Indigenous perspective to typically Eurocentric subgenres of science fiction. It is a look toward daunting possible futures while holding on to the meaningful values that our people have learned from the land and from our Ancestors.

JORDANNA GEORGE, ARTIST
Tsleil-Waututh Territory, Vancouver Area
April 2021

# Me Tomorrow—
# Paint It Red

**DARREL J. MCLEOD**
Writer, Educator & Activist

*The future of humankind lies waiting for those who will
come to understand their lives and take up responsibilities
to all living things. Who will listen to the trees, the animals
and birds, the voices of the places of the land? As the long-
forgotten peoples of respective continents rise and begin to
reclaim their ancient heritage, they will discover the meaning of the land of their ancestors. That is when the invaders
of the North American continent will finally discover that for
this land, God is red.*
—Vine Deloria Jr., *God Is Red*

THIS WISDOM FROM VINE DELORIA JR. PARALLELS ALMOST
exactly the wisdom my mother, Bertha Dora Cardinal,
passed on to me repeatedly in the wee hours (ironically,
while inebriated) with respect to dealing with a world that
she viewed as increasingly hostile to the culture and future
of our people, Nehiyawak. In a careful and astute way,
Mother instilled in me a *méfiance* of Western religion and
world views, and of the increasingly dominant and repres-
sive culture of Canada.

Mother planted the seeds of distrust, apprehension and fearlessness, fomenting in me an urgent desire to spurn a world view that had been forced upon us, so that as an adult I could rediscover our Nehiyaw cosmovision. Fortunately for me, those seeds took root early in my life and over the last four decades my ruminations have led me to the thinking captured in this essay (which represents my first attempt at articulating it). I've blended the four elements of the Indigenous cosmovision with the four directions of the medicine wheel.

## EARTH

### Spiritual

Mother Earth—the Pachamama—is everything to Indigenous Peoples. She does not belong to us; rather, we belong to her, and how our relationship with her evolves will determine our future. Over generations, the acculturation by dominating forces has eroded our direct and innate connection with Mother Earth to the point that many of us find ourselves quite removed, literally and/or figuratively, from our place of origin, sometimes feeling like we're in a true physical exile or simply forced to live and strive somewhere else, away, for the sake of survival and expediency. Increasingly, Indigenous people will re-establish the connection with our places of origin, our original birthplaces—the land, water, air and fire there—and make our presence known. We will ensure that our cosmovision is known to our youth, and they, in turn, strengthened and emboldened, will change the world—for the better.

Physical

Western political entities have asserted ownership of lands, territories and entire continents through a process that in modern times would be seen as bullying and aggression: the dispossession of lands through physical domination, starvation and the imposition of a foreign legal tradition, including a system of registration of land titles that has come to be sacrosanct in modern societies. But the original basis of land title in the Western world is farcical: a king, queen or some other aristocrat, through an instrument of their own design, declared lands, territories or entire continents unoccupied and then asserted ownership of them. Subsequently, he or she, as a benevolent despot, would grant a secondary type of ownership to his or her loyal subjects in the form of a lesser title, the most common of which is fee simple title. It's time for a complete repudiation of this entrenched system of land ownership.

In Canada and other so-called commonwealth countries, we must reject and put on its ear this legal tradition that runs completely counter to Indigenous principles. Even in Indigenous societies where leaders—chiefs or *caciques*—were allowed to accumulate wealth or assert a type of large-scale ownership over lands and resources, it was all within a system of shared trust, where wealth was regularly redistributed.

Since time immemorial, the earth has provided us with all that we need to flourish as Indigenous people and live long and healthy lives. Young Indigenous scientists are exploring elements of our traditional diet that are missing in the present day and are bringing back traditional food sources that will help us to combat conditions like diabetes, obesity and mental illness. Not only do we need to avoid foods with a high glycemic index, for example, but we also need to reincorporate healing foods like wild berries (such as cranberries and salal In North America) and the perennial sunflower, apparently known in Cree as *askipaw* or *skibwan*, but now referred to as the Jerusalem artichoke, which is high in protein and potassium, helps with insulin production and lowers cholesterol levels (of course, tribes in parts of the world other than North America will have their own traditional foods, which kept them healthy and strong but may have been abandoned in favour of the foods of a colonizing force).

In addition to nutrition, the earth also provides us with medicines we need to maintain and enhance our physical and spiritual well-being. Indigenous Peoples all over the world have ancient knowledge of the plant and animal parts used in these medicines. The resurgence we're seeing in the use of our medicines will continue and expand, as will the borrowing of this important part of our culture by the mainstream. Indigenous scholars and leaders will demand recognition of the contribution Indigenous Peoples have made to modern technology and will hopefully use both legal and moral persuasion to convince corporate players like Big Pharma to provide retroactive profit-sharing for the Indigenous knowledge they've turned into products that have generated huge profits for them. Prime examples are digitalis and yew bark.

### Intellectual

Every Indigenous culture has a story about the origin of their race. As time moves on, we will repudiate the mythology of Adam and Eve in favour of our own creation stories. Our young people are already debunking the Christian doctrine of original sin and we will continue to do so until we have removed ourselves from the trappings of imposed religion. This repudiation will include the complete refusal, for once and for all, of the notion that we migrated to our territories. For certain there was movement and migration prior to colonization of Indigenous societies, but we didn't come from another continent—none of our creation stories say that, and as we take back the thinking on this matter from anthropologists and other theorists, we will be even stronger in our connection with the lands with which we are inextricably linked.

Fortunately, there are examples of the restoration and recognition of this fundamental connection between Indigenous Peoples and the Pachamama. The most recent powerful example I'm aware of is the Roger Williams case, won by the Tsilhqot'in in the Supreme Court of Canada. This is the first case where a First Nation won clear title to their territory, where "title" actually means the Tsilhqot'in have outright ownership—the use and administration of a great portion of the lands that constitute their traditional territory, rather than the simple usufructuary rights typically attributed to Aboriginal title. This new reality of the Tsilhqot'in represents a type of de facto Indigenous sovereignty for the Tsilhqot'in within Canada. Since European contact, Tsilhqot'in leaders have been steadfast in their relationship with Mother Earth—the land where their people originated—and they were meticulous in documenting and maintaining this tight connection. This fact has paid off tremendously, against all odds.

North of the 60th parallel in Canada, both the Sahtú Dene and the Inuit of Nunavut have maintained their powerful relationship with their territories as well and, as a result, now exert meaningful, true sovereignty over their lands and territories. These trail-blazing nations are setting examples for the future, a future where everything has to be on the table in negotiation or other methods of asserting Indigenous rights with existing state governments, including, for example, the numbered treaties in Canada, which have never been fully implemented.

Emotional

There has been a crisis of suicide among Indigenous youth around the world, in some places more than others. In Canada, the Indigenous suicide rate is known to be much higher than that of the general population. When I worked with Indigenous people in Argentina and other countries, I was shocked and saddened to learn that they have the same issue. I believe this is happening because of the incredible erosion of our culture, languages and sovereignty, starting with the false assertions, mentioned earlier, that we came from someplace else, and that we too are subject to a creation myth we cannot relate to. As we take back the thinking on this and strengthen our cultures and restore our cosmovision, our youth will become stronger and triumphant and will astonish society with their accomplishments in the arts and sciences, as well as in life overall.

We are and always have been "earthy" people—never in denial or ashamed of our humanity, our physical bodies or sexuality. Gender diversity and variations in sexual orientation were viewed as normal, and in most Indigenous cultures those who were non-binary in their sexuality were given a place of honour and particular roles in society. Mainstream society (at least in North America) is slowly getting back to this, as are Indigenous societies, largely thanks to our youth, who are not simply expanding the thinking in this area but rather are blowing it up altogether. We will bring our leaders onside with the traditional views and practices in this regard and will drive progress in this area in mainstream society.

My last thought in this section will be a bit controversial for some readers. Indigenous people who have remained strongly connected to their territories often have a darker complexion than other Indigenous people—possibly because there has been less intermarriage or mixing of their genes with European settlers. My experience has been that these people suffer more discrimination than Indigenous people who have a lighter complexion. I've observed that these proud carriers of Indigenous culture and languages experience discrimination even at the hands of other Indigenous people, and this must stop. In the next couple of decades, the Indigenous population, writ large, will begin to honour and even revere our relations who have always remained close to Mother Earth and who, as a result of this and other factors, may have a darker complexion.

## AIR—WIND

### Spiritual

Imagine my surprise when the Mapuche people I was visiting in Argentina invited me into the courtyard of their traditional ruka to participate in a smudge ceremony. I shouldn't have been surprised by this, but I was. The herbs my Mapuche relations used weren't the sweetgrass or sage I was used to back home, but their pungent aroma and its effects on me were just as powerful. Scientists are exploring something Indigenous Peoples around the world have believed for countless generations: smoke from certain herbs has a cleansing and healing effect. Some scientists have even begun to refer to smoke from burning sage as "medicinal smoke." For Indigenous Peoples, and likely for everyone, smudging with traditional herbs will become part of a daily self-care routine, and this practice will continue to spread into the mainstream population.

Hot, humid air combined with the burning of traditional herbs in a sweat lodge–type ceremony intensifies the healing effects of burning traditional herbs, and this practice is becoming universal among Indigenous Peoples around the world.

### · Intellectual

Indigenous Peoples will increasingly demand a seat at the table in discussions related to air quality, and we will become leaders in finding ways to minimize our "carbon footprint" in the world. While global travel by the rest of humanity peaks, we will remain content and secure in our own ecosystems and natural biomes, even though the rest of the world will be increasingly mystified by how we can stay within something like a five-hundred-kilometre radius around our territories and feel we're not missing out on anything.

Physical

Within their legal framework of ownership of the world, Western societies include ownership of the air and, within what is a fee simple–like type of tenure, they grant limited control over air one hundred feet above the ground, appropriating for themselves ownership, administration and control of air space above 100 feet. This appropriation of the ownership of the skies has led to the troublesome situation the world finds itself in. Indigenous Peoples have never been consulted in the setting of things like emission standards, or control of or restrictions on the amount or type of air travel that is allowed in and around their territories. Indigenous Peoples around the world will demand increased influence on and say in these matters. Traditional knowledge and wisdom, as counterintuitive as it may seem, will enter into play here.

It is early days in the investigation of another type of problematic saturation of air space—the saturation of the biosphere with different frequencies and types of electromagnetic radiation. Indigenous Peoples can and will increasingly be the stewards of the air around us and of the amount of electromagnetic radiation in our territories, given our close relationship with nature. Increasingly, Indigenous people will study and participate in the sciences that will complement so beautifully their traditional and intuitive knowledge.

Telepathy is a medium that was used between Indigenous people, though it is very hard to illustrate this. I strongly believe that telepathy as a means of efficient and healthy communication will make a strong return, and this will begin with us and will displace the mounting reliance on electronic forms of communication.

### Emotional

There is an Indigenous revolution happening in the arts, and it's occurring around the world. Indigenous artists of all media and forms of expression are taking up more space each year and gaining positive attention, and this will continue, including with regard to humour. Humour may seem trivial and unimportant in Western culture, but it has always been a cornerstone of Indigenous culture. Deliberate comedy is a field more Indigenous artists will engage in and excel at. Speaking of which, did you hear the one about . . .

### FIRE

### Spiritual

Fire has always been at the centre of Indigenous culture and is, of course, used to heat the rocks—the grandfathers— used in ceremonies like the sweat lodge ceremony. Fire allows the transition from one state of matter to another— ice can become water, which in turn becomes vapour. Solid rocks can become molten rocks. We will return to the magical and mystical source of heat energy.

## Intellectual

It will become increasingly clear how societies with more advanced technology related to fire—more "fire power," if you will—dominated and massacred Indigenous people around the world at various points in time. Indigenous Peoples, tired and enraged at being on the receiving end of this violence, will decide that it's time to use this ancient power source in our own defence. We will skilfully and strategically increase our own fire power, but unlike other societies, we will use it in self-defence, and not for aggression or conquest, or to satiate greed. The Oka crisis in Quebec, driven by dishonesty and greed, was truly the first situation I'm aware of anywhere where a dominant society backed down from their aggressive militarized stance because the Indigenous people they were trying to suppress had significant and real fire power in the form of modern weapons.

Hopefully this unfortunate, but necessary, partial militarization will be a collective effort where select tribes in various countries equip and train a type of elite militia that can be dispersed to places where a state government or corporate interest has decided to use force to dominate a community or tribe. Related to this, Indigenous people could develop a mechanism I'll call a "reverse intelligence network" to monitor state governments and multinational corporations to keep one step ahead of any emerging plans for repression. This elite force would also investigate crimes against Indigenous people, whether directed against individuals or groups, and demand justice and retribution via the appropriate national or international bodies.

## Physical

The traditional Indigenous use of fire for ecosystem management will make a huge comeback and will be utilized to reduce the incidence of wildfires in different parts of the world.

Nutrition—fire for the body and spirit—will shift. Indigenous Peoples will increasingly understand what type of diet works for our bodies, which will likely be something akin to the paleo diet. However, our diet will increasingly become more plant-based and, as a result, our longevity will return to the high levels it was precontact, and even higher.

The use of solar energy will revolutionize the lives of Indigenous Peoples who have always lived in isolated settings, some of whom may never have had electricity, running water or other modern conveniences. With their recently gained access to electricity, telecommunications and electronic media, these Indigenous Peoples will interact with the world around them more, but on their own terms, sharing knowledge, culture and other aspects of their worldview as they see fit. They will also benefit from Western education as they deem appropriate, without losing their youth to the dominant societies around them and, most importantly, without being acculturated.

Emotional

Fire is the source of warmth and healing. Following a series of pandemics that will occur after the COVID-19 pandemic, people will be less and less prone to have physical contact with each other for affection or sex. Procreation will increasingly be done by artificial insemination. Indigenous Peoples will resist this trend and be among the few races that continue to enjoy genuine physical contact between humans. This will enhance their vitality as peoples, while that of others diminishes.

The disruption caused by generations of families attending residential school has caused a great chill in the parent-child relationship in Indigenous families, and increasingly natural human warmth and instinctual love is already healing this issue and will continue to do so. The healing power and warmth of fire will help to address the suicide crisis mentioned earlier. Multi-generational trauma takes decades to heal, but within the next twenty to fifty years, more healing will occur and Indigenous Peoples around the world will thrive.

## WATER

Spiritual, Intellectual, Emotional and Physical

I've written this entire essay while seated on or above *la orilla* of Banderas Bay in Mexico, listening to the waves of the Pacific Ocean, trying to discern the ancient knowledge and wisdom the water imparts to anyone who will take time to listen—time to let it permeate their being. Each day before writing, I've done the traditional ceremony my mother taught me to do on arrival at any body of water. I wade into the bay, ankle- or knee-deep, and pull handfuls of water up over my bare arms and then wash my face and neck with it. Then I stand still, raise my hands in awe, and glance around while giving thanks and asking the water for its blessing.

Water is the giver of life, and I've always been drawn to it—sought to live in a place where a lake, river or sea is visible or, even better, both visible and audible. My mother used to say that I was conceived on the banks of the Nechako River, and in my late twenties, life's circumstances brought me back to that place, like the salmon of that river system returning to its place of creation to spawn (except I didn't have the good fortune to do that there). I may have been conceived on the banks of the Nechako, but I was born in the neighbouring watershed, near the Athabasca River, and raised along the Salteaux, Slave, Athabasca and Makhabn (Bow) Rivers. I have lived on the shores of Stuart Lake, Shuswap Lake and now the Salish Sea. Without these bodies of water, I would be nothing. They've comforted me, nourished me and inspired me, and they continue to. I was never taught this, but wherever I go, intuitively, I pay homage to the nearby bodies of water, and this brings me great satisfaction and peace, and also seems to strike a chord with those who are present as witnesses.

In addition to living near these bodies of water, I've had the good fortune to visit the Sahtú region in the Far North. The Sahtú, also known as Great Bear Lake, is apparently the twelfth largest body of water in the world. The people who have inhabited the Sahtú region since time immemorial, the Sahtú Dene, believe that lakes like the

Sahtú are the lungs of Mother Earth and the guardians of this one huge source of oxygen (science confirms that the phytoplankton in oceans and lakes is one of the planet's most important producers of oxygen). The Dene prophet Ayah predicted that one day there will be a great drought, at which time the world will look to the Sahtú as a crucial water source. The Sahtú Dene defend and protect the Sahtú with the well-being of the entire planet and all of its inhabitants in mind.

There are many other important lakes in North America, although not as large as the Sahtú, and Indigenous Peoples are guardians and stewards of those lakes, just as the Dene are of the Sahtú. This role will become increasingly important.

In the 1990s, in an amazingly beautiful part of Nuu-chah-nulth territory called Clayoquot Sound on the west coast of Canada, there was an intense conflict between industry, government and the local First Nations (and their allies) related to the logging of an old-growth forest. Hoping to find a solution to the stalemate, the provincial government of BC decided to convene what it called the Clayoquot Sound Scientific Panel. On this panel, Nuu-chah-nulth Elders were given the same standing as PhD-level scientists. After months of working together, the Elders and scientists gained tremendous respect for each other, and together over the course of a few years they concluded that an ecosystem approach to environmental management was the only sustainable method possible. To this day, I am not aware of such a progressive body being established anywhere else, a body in which Western scientific knowledge is paired with Indigenous knowledge to design a sustainable approach to environmental management. Indigenous people will increasingly demand that their knowledge be given standing equal to the so-called scientific knowledge of Western society, as occurred in this situation. And, increasingly, scientists will validate that knowledge.

In the late 1980s, when I was a school principal in Yekooche First Nation in northern BC, I intuitively had insight into the importance of ecosystems. In establishing the curriculum for the school, I scrapped the government-prescribed program of studies to instead focus on local knowledge—to help the students learn about the ecosystem they were heirs to, the one they would one day, as adults, become the stewards of. We mapped the streams, rivers and lakes within the territory and then beyond to show how their ecosystem connected with others. With the Elders and other adults of the community, we explored how that ecosystem has provided sustenance for the people of Yekooche since the beginning of time, and we explored the traditional names of the lakes, streams and rivers in the local ecosystem. I believe it was during my time with the Yekooche people that I came to appreciate the sacredness of bodies of water and their importance to human survival and sustenance. Whenever I mention a river or lake in my writing now, I strive to find and use the Indigenous name for it. This returning to the Indigenous names of bodies of water and landmarks is critical in the process of repudiating government ownership and title over these bodies of water (and their beds and shorelines), and of renewing or continuing our role as stewards and protectors of the ecosystem(s) within our territories.

Historically, Indigenous people were great swimmers, and in some parts of the world they still are, but somehow we've lost this skill. We need to get back to this intimate, immersive relationship with water, and we will. Given the number of Indigenous communities located near rivers, lakes and seas, schools and non-profit organizations should make swimming and water safety instruction a priority, and Indigenous leaders should embrace this. Learning how to swim gives a quantum lift to a child's self-esteem, and the health benefits of swimming are tremendous. Initiatives in this area will result in something unheard of to date: Indigenous people will become champion swimmers and divers, just as we are increasingly excelling in other athletic fields.

My spirit sister, Dr. Kathy Absolon, a Midewin, taught me that I should always have a glass of water present in my personal smudge ceremonies, and now I do. That glass of water makes all four elements present in my ceremony—earth, air, fire and water—and sets the foundation for me to briefly visit the spiritual realm and spend time with the Ancestors of the place I'm in at any point in time. For the remainder of my life, in my ceremonies I will pray that the positive vision I've articulated here becomes a reality in the next twenty to fifty years for all my Indigenous relations in Canada and around the world. I invite everyone reading these words to join me in this prayer. Indigenous people have only just begun to reclaim our space in the broader human context, and I'm filled with optimism and hope about our future. Let's paint it red.

# Our Future Is Young, Educated and Relational

**MINADOO MAKWA BASKIN**
Student & Leader
and
**DR. CYNDY BASKIN**
Writer, Researcher & Educator

## INTRODUCTION

**M**AKWA AND CYNDY WONDERED WHETHER TO WRITE about Indigenous Peoples twenty years or fifty years from now. Although Cyndy believes that what she is predicting is more likely fifty years from now, she wanted twenty years because in fifty she will be dead and so not physically present to see if anything she predicts becomes reality (LOL). However, she invites readers to look at what she writes from either a twenty-year or fifty-year walk in the future.

In twenty years, Makwa will be forty-one years old, the age that his mother, Cyndy, was when she gave birth to him. He will be a Ryerson University and First Nations Technical Institute graduate holding a bachelor's degree in public administration and Indigenous governance, and a master's degree (he is not certain in what discipline at this time), and looking to pursue a PhD (if he doesn't have it by then). Around this time, Makwa hopes to have a well-established municipal political platform based on community development. This would be specific to non-Métis, Indigenous-mixed peoples, whom Makwa has found are often left out of both Canadian and Indigenous innovation plans pertaining to cultural and economic development. The big picture, and where Makwa hopes his ambitions will lead him, is working for all Indigenous communities in Canada as a liaison atop a reformed Indigenous Services Canada, with a focus on Indigenous-led resource management and sustainable protocols. Much like Cyndy, Makwa aims to continue educating himself in the social, economic and political realms in order to continue lobbying on behalf of Indigenous communities for cycle-ending assistance programs for and administered by Indigenous Peoples. Most importantly, Makwa hopes to be a good father, building on the importance of academia instilled in him by his mother, Cyndy, and the importance of core Indigenous cultural knowledge (particularly Anishinaabe) instilled in him by his father, Marcel.

Twenty years from now, Cyndy will have retired from teaching in post-secondary education, but she will still be working, only not as much. She will continue to write and teach in other ways. She will be a mentor to many young Indigenous people. She will be healthy and active, still meditating and involved with her many grandchildren. If you decide to look at this writing as being about fifty years from now, Cyndy will no longer be in the physical realm but will certainly be watching closely what is happening on the planet from the spirit world.

Makwa envisions himself living his elder years with as much zest as Cyndy has. At that time, he will surely be retired from a life of politics and, although he would like to be an adviser to the next generation, he understands the importance of fresh ideas from fresh minds. Still, Makwa will fulfill this purpose by serving as a board member to various Indigenous organizations, as an investor in Indigenous businesses and, quite possibly, as Cyndy did before, as an educator. Makwa will spend his retirement either funding or writing grant applications for the implementation of community farms to tackle Indigenous food insecurity in a multitude of ways, while contributing to a global information repository of Indigenous knowledges.

The following is based on a conversation that Makwa and Cyndy recently had about their thoughts on the future for Indigenous Peoples.

## OUR FUTURE IS HOPEFUL

CYNDY: Readers of this chapter will notice that I am hopeful about the future for Indigenous Peoples. I am hopeful because, despite all the challenges and struggles we continue to face today, we have recently made progress in creating better spaces and places for Indigenous Peoples. We have done so in the areas of music and other forms of the arts, within academia, and in creating culture-based services that support individuals, families and communities. We have lawyers, judges, senators, psychiatrists, doctors and fashion designers, and their numbers continue to grow. I am hopeful because I see so much hard work being done for the good of the whole, often with personal sacrifice, facing the risks involved when taking a stand on what is important and keeping our good minds on a better world for the next seven generations.

I am hopeful because young Indigenous people around the globe are in contact now, sometimes in person, but mostly through technology, such as Zoom, Facebook and online video games. Our Ancestors, such as those of the Hopi Nation, saw this coming as they talked about a giant spider web that would connect people from around the world. Is it a coincidence that the internet is called the World Wide Web? I don't think so. Through social media via the internet, youth from the four directions can share their stories, recognize their vast similarities despite geography, and develop relationships that can last a lifetime. Politicized youth can come together as a unified global population, pressuring others to open their eyes and minds to what Indigenous Peoples have known since the beginning of time.

The internet can also be vital to Indigenous rights movements, allowing youth to participate in dialogue that can create a better understanding of their identities. It can be used as a tool to connect with other Indigenous groups, spread solidarity and give them greater political clout. An example of the use of the internet to educate people across the globe is the grassroots movement, Idle No More. Since 2012, 400,000 people and hundreds of local Indigenous-led agencies and organizations self-organized around the world under the hashtag #IdleNoMore. Using its website, many YouTube videos and a Facebook account, Idle No More works through solidarity actions on an international level while connecting the most remote First Nations communities with each other, with urbanized Indigenous people and with the non-Indigenous population. Fluent in social media and new technologies, this movement upholds Indigenous rights and the protection of land, water and sky. As technology advances in the future, and our young people grow up immersed in it, they will have powerful tools to go beyond what Idle No More has achieved in continuing to connect, educate and organize both Indigenous and non-Indigenous peoples.

Another medium, music, has always been a way of relaying messages and, through the internet, this has become easy, providing opportunities for many Indigenous youth to share their work like never before. Artists like A Tribe Called Red have gained an international following that continues to build a peaceful revolution through their genre-bending mix of electronic dance music, hip-hop and First Nations traditions. Sharing songs, such as "Land Back," and partnering with diverse musicians, like Muslim hip-hop artist Yasiin Bey, Tribe promotes a combination of political stances and unity among all.

I am hopeful because I, and many around me, refuse to be immobilized by fear and sadness, and instead we are using our justifiable anger and passion to make positive change. Without hope, I might as well lie down and die because I would be of no use to anyone.

MAKWA: I, too, see a rich future for Indigenous Peoples, at least in the scope of Canada. For myself, I draw hope from those past generations who laid the foundation for us to fight for social equality and financial equity for Indigenous Canadians. Doing the work while honouring my Clan teachings, my grandfathers and the present collective is what propels me to carry that work into the next stage. Along the way, I have hit these "checkpoints" where I look around and see my Indigenous colleagues succeeding, including Indigenous-mixed Peoples like myself, all of whom are well established in their communities as teachers, healers, staff carriers and pipe carriers, but also as nurses, educators and boxers.

In both a national and a global movement, Indigenous Peoples have at last sparked the conversation of Indigenous autonomy in multiple nation-states. In Canada specifically, we are starting to move away from legislation created *for* Indigenous people into that created *by* Indigenous people. I think the future will be a time of bolstering that ideology and what that looks like not just for Indigenous people but for all Canadians. The importance of autonomy was driven home for me while attending the Ryerson-FNTI (First Nations Technical Institute) partnership program in public administration and governance. Here, for the first time, I was being educated by culturally knowledgeable Indigenous professors who saw us all as the future, those who would create world bridges or carry the torches to set the seventh fire.

## THE FULFILLMENT OF PROPHECIES

CYNDY: When I think about the future, the first thing that arises are the many prophecies that Indigenous Peoples have talked about for a long time. Unlike most prophecies, those of Indigenous Nations are not necessarily about an inevitable apocalypse (although at the time of writing this, we are living with COVID-19, which I refer to as the zombie apocalypse) or the end of the world. Instead, the fate of humankind and the world is in the control of human beings. Indigenous prophecies speak about choice, which is critical to what the future will look like.

Many of these prophecies refer to the seventh generation or the seventh fire. For example, the Onkwehonwe tell of a time when, after living with the newcomers for seven generations, the trees, birds and fish will begin to die. Animals and people will be born with deformities. Huge stone monsters will rip open the earth. Eventually, people will grow ashamed of how they have treated the earth, their mother and provider. Then the Onkwehonwe will rise and demand that their rights and stewardship over the land be respected and restored. Importantly, other people will finally see the wisdom of the Onkwehonwe and turn to them for guidance and direction on saving Mother Earth. Children and youth are the seventh generation, and they will decide what to do.

Similarly, the Anishinaabe Nation tells of a time that they call the seventh fire, which will bring a new generation that will seek knowledge, pick up the teachings that have been put aside and take action on the state of the earth. Most people do not know this, but these Anishinaabe prophecies originated with the Mi'kmaq Nation, who promised the Anishinaabe protection as they moved from the Atlantic coast through what are now Quebec and Ontario. The seventh fire also speaks to the descendants of the newcomers, telling them that they will have a choice between two roads. One road will lead to the eighth and final fire, a time of liberation and healing. The other road will continue to lead people along the path of destroying the earth. Like the Onkwehonwe prophecy, this one too speaks of other people reaching out to the Anishinaabe to help them save the planet.

Mi'kmaq prophecies focus on all Indigenous Nations coming together with the purpose of leading the rest of the people of the world. They speak of putting aside differences, considering what we have in common and joining together. They emphasize the fact that while new knowledge and wisdom will come out of this, it must be based on the old teachings if we are to save the planet from destruction. We will know we are in this final stage when the Creator takes the earth in both hands and shakes it violently. This will be the warning of the coming of great misery and destitution for all people. However, we will have a choice: allow this destruction to happen or prevent it. We can achieve the latter if we heed the wisdom of the Elders, who have the abilities to restore balance in the world.

The Lakota have a prophecy about a giant black snake that tries to cross a mighty river. If this snake crosses the river, the end of the world will begin. If it is prevented from crossing, then a new time of co-operation and peace will emerge. It is a hawk and an eagle that help the people kill the black snake, which is viewed as a sign of racial unity.

The current generation is living with the signs of the choice we must make in the future: stone monsters are bulldozers and other machines that tear open Mother Earth. The black snake is oil. Preventing the snake from crossing the river are the protests at Standing Rock, North Dakota, against the Dakota Access Pipeline, and in Wet'su-wet'en First Nation territory in British Columbia against the Coastal Gaslink pipeline. Indigenous Peoples the world over are standing up for their rights and the protection of the land, and this will grow exponentially in the future.

Today, it is mostly young people who are protecting the water and land, not only through their creations via technology, social media, music and video, but more significantly through their learning and actions—like young activists, seventeen-year-old Autumn Peltier, who fights for access to clean water; Xiuhtezcatl Martinez, the twenty-one-year-old youth director of Earth Guardians, which is made up of young activists, artists and musicians from across the globe who are stepping up as leaders and collaborating to defend the planet; and Helena Gualinga, a nineteen-year-old from the Ecuadorian Amazon who has been fighting against climate change since she was a child.

It will be the youth of the seventh generation who lead all the people along the road to the eighth fire. I can only imagine the access to knowledge and the tools that the seventh generation will invent for this purpose.

MAKWA: There is certainly no denying the accuracy of the fifth to eighth fire prophecies in predicting the negative effects of colonialism on Indigenous Peoples and the earth they strive to protect. Following that line of thought, I believe it is fitting that the responsibility for a just future falls on the youth, and in some specific ways, on urban Indigenous youth. Urban centres provide the foundation for unique alliances and resources, not found in my First Nation, to be leveraged. However, before we ignite that eighth fire, before the seventh Haudenosaunee generation rises, before the descent of the Nêhiyaw Rainbow Prophecy, or the eighth star of the bear constellation signals the Lakota Wakinyapi, we must return to the land. Onwegitchigewin, or "things to come," has always guided the Anishinaabe. The Elders have spoken about how many sicknesses would plague Indigenous Nations and then, when no one listened, that sickness would spread further. Of course, now we are fighting COVID-19, which affects everyone on the planet. Sickness has always played a role in the aftermath of hoarding resources and causing damage to the earth. What strikes me the most is that weaknesses within the global economy have been brought to light and the narrative of "natural disasters" cannot be the same again.

Anishinaabe protection of the land, or Mashkikiiaki'ing, teaches us that there are no natural disasters. Everything has a cause and effect, as we are all related to one another in the four directions associated with the medicine wheel. This much has been realized, but the preventive work to combat negative outcomes as prophesied may not be done until the earth nears its cosmic end. In Indigenous fashion, as we experience situations resembling an end, in the future, we as a people, will experience a new relationship with the ancestors, where hopefully we can all be guided to a path of mino-pimâtisiwin, the good life. But to do so, the Elders have said that we must isolate on the land and cultivate our medicines, a double entendre, I am sure, meaning we must research the medicinal plants but also look inward to find our roots as medicine people.

Once, when working at a landscaping job I despised, I had an altercation with my employer that called for a mediation meeting. This person hired an Indigenous woman to do the mediating, to make me feel more "comfortable." The mediator said something along the lines of "it's your responsibility to educate these people, as they could not learn themselves." This left a sour taste in my mouth, but looking back, I see that Canadians cannot learn and unlearn for themselves, under capitalistic stress, what Indigenous Peoples have studied for centuries to combat the negative effects of what has been taught by this economic ideology.

So now I see that my future is to educate and push for the acceptance of Indigenous knowledges, not for one specific group of Indigenous people, but rather for the earth and the Creator. For myself, I look to Midewiwin (medicine society) and, although it is hard at times, I place that above human wants or needs. My future will focus on how I can bring myself back to Midewiwin practices, as well as the environments that I live and work in.

## CANADA NEEDS US

CYNDY: If we see the future of a country as being its youth, then Canada's future is increasingly Indigenous. The Indigenous youth population is growing at three times the national average and we have more children than anyone else—go, Indigenous Peoples! In 2016, 29.2 percent of First Nations, 22.3 percent of Métis, 33 percent of Inuit and 16.4 percent of non-Indigenous people were under the age of fourteen.[1] We will be a force to be reckoned with, but for this to be a force for positive change and economic growth, we all need to take appropriate action. Canada needs Indigenous youth because the rest of the population is aging and a lot of them will be retiring over the next decades.[2]

.................

1      Statistics Canada, "Share (in Percentage) of the Population Aged 0 to 14 years and 65 years and over by Aboriginal Identity, Canada, 2016." https://www.statcan.gc.ca/n1/daily-quotidien /171025/cg-a001-eng.htm.

2      "More Canadians Are 65 and Over Than Under Age 15, StatsCan Says," CBC News (September 29, 2015). https://www.cbc.ca /news/business/statistics-canada-seniors-1.3248295.

So old white people plus thousands of Indigenous youth equals Canada needing the latter to sustain the economy in the future. For me, as an educator, this highlights the importance of post-secondary education for youth, so they become the engineers, doctors, entrepreneurs, political leaders and scientists of the future, not only to save Canada from itself but to positively impact Indigenous communities. Already Indigenous youth are standing up to oppressive policies, pushing through a racist world and holding their heads up with confidence for their people and communities. These actions will grow significantly over the next decades. This makes me think of a back-to-the-future kind of idea. When the newcomers came to Turtle Island, they needed Indigenous Peoples to teach them how to survive here. They will need us in the future for the same reasons.

Young Indigenous people will be the ones making significant changes in their communities. They will not stand by and accept things the way they are. They will raise their voices and they will fight not only for themselves but for the next seven generations coming after them and for their Ancestors, who did not have the power to change their circumstances. Like my son, future youth will only have their traditional names, which come from the Ancestors and give us purpose and direction as to what we are to do in the lifetime we are in. Minadoo Makwa, Spirit-Bear in Anishinaabemowin, was passed on to my son from the Ancestors through our Elder and friend, Edna Manitowabi, whose daughter was fasting in the bush when my son was born. A young bear visited her one day and, when her mother checked on her and heard about this, she knew the name that was waiting for my son to take. In a traditional naming ceremony, Edna announced my son's name, which is about bringing the strong spirit of the bear into one's life as a protector and healer of the people. The spirit of Makwa's name grows as he does. The spirit world will provide young people with the knowledge of who they are so they will have the guidance, direction and strength they need to create the future that Makwa and I are writing about.

I see Indigenous youth adapting the stories and teachings of their Elders into experimental digital media, such as video games, creating movies shot in a virtual world with avatars as actors, and inventing alternatives to sustainable energy extraction that will not harm the environment. I see them belonging in both their First Nations communities and in urban centres. They will have choices and hope; they will make their dreams come true; they will nurture their talents and intelligence. In twenty years, Indigenous youth employment will be on par with or better than the Canadian average. Canadian society will shine a light on their successes instead of focusing on lack of education, poverty, gangs and suicide rates. They will be engaged, articulate and forward-thinking warriors. They will come up with resolutions to the longstanding grievances between Indigenous Peoples and the Canadian state and public, such as treaty obligations. This will be their truth and reconciliation.

MAKWA: The concept of reconciliation, as put forth by the Truth and Reconciliation Commission and the Government of Canada, is bittersweet to me. Although it is a huge step forward to require private corporations and Crown corporations to involve and consult with Indigenous Nations, this is only a step. It is interesting growing up as an Indigenous person, both academically and spiritually, in a time when some Indigenous academics and activists are steeped in "reconciliation is dead" and "allyship as the ship that never sailed" rhetoric. A lot of important conversations relating to Indigenous autonomy and what that means for Canadian economics, politics and society with its many intersections will be a focus in the future. If reconciliation comes about, it will be tangible change in Indigenous communities that comes from a partnership between traditional Indigenous governments and the federal government. The resurgence of Indigenous knowledges in an Indigenous-controlled environment will have many benefits for Indigenous Peoples, but for Canada, it is the key to sustainability in the resource sector.

In the future, the paradigm of equity will shift. With Canada depending on Indigenous Peoples, instead of Indigenous Peoples depending on Canada through social services and funding, the conversations will change for the next generation. By going back to the land and to Indigenous roots of governance, curating practices and education, we as Indigenous Peoples will return to the societal roles that once ensured our survival. The future will be Indigenous Peoples in Canada realizing that our alliance is with Mother Earth, our obligation to her, not to cleaning up or reconciling the federal government's transgressions.

## EDUCATION

CYNDY: I want to write more here about education for Indigenous youth because it is so critical for our future. It is mind-blowing to me that current "school structures are fundamentally based on an antiquated system established in the late 1800s."[3] Clearly, we need an upgrade here that will create a shift to excitement when working with Indigenous students and parents, rather than perpetuating a dismal situation based on a "racism of low expectations," meaning that these students are prevented from achieving higher graduation rates and entering post-secondary education because the system does not expect much from them.[4]

Indigenous youth will enter post-secondary education in large numbers. They will be visible and demand that the disciplines they choose, such as governance and medicine, include Indigenous knowledges. They will not allow Canadians to speak about them as living only in the past. They will challenge their educators to do better. They will do so not merely for their own well-being, but to help their communities.

We have made many strides in education, but my generation's work needs to be built on. Like both my Indigenous and Buddhist teachings (I became a Buddhist and Bodhisattva several years ago) and the message of writer and professor Yuval Noah Harari, I know that the only constant in this world is change. Thus, in the future, education will be more about understanding than simply receiving information. It will be about wanting to understand the world,

...................

3    H.H. Jacobs, "Introduction," in *Curriculum 21: Essential Education for a Changing World*, ed. H.H. Jacobs (Association for Supervision and Curriculum Development, 2010), 1.

4    Auditor General of British Columbia, *An Audit of the Education of Aboriginal Students in the BC Public School System* (Victoria, BC: Office of the Auditor General, 2015). https://www.bcauditor.com/sites/default/files/publications/reports/OAGBC%20Aboriginal%20Education%20Report_FINAL.pdf.

rather than controlling it. Individuality will be revealed as the myth it is because nothing is ever done by only one person. Learning will be accompanied by a focus on resiliency and how to sustain positive mental health. Children and youth will be investing more time in revealing their biases and becoming more critical of the sources of information provided to them. Hence, they will learn how to investigate and verify what they are being taught and who is teaching it to them. They will be more in tune with their bodies and the mental reactions they have to people and occurrences around them because their education will include learning how to meditate. This will lead to a greater understanding of themselves as connected with everyone and everything else. When they know these things and can see how their minds work, it will be "the first step toward ceasing to generate more suffering" in themselves and the world around them.[5] It will also avert the algorithms making up their minds for them (LOL)![6]

Ceasing to generate more suffering through education particularly applies to the helping professions, such as social work. This is a profession that has been used as a tool of colonization for decades; I can personally attest to this, as I worked as a front-line practitioner for many years and am now a social work educator. Most Indigenous social workers go into the area of child welfare with the goal of changing the system to better meet the needs of Indigenous families, but they are constrained by Western policies and legislation that often place unsurmountable obstacles in their way.

..................

5    Yuval Noah Harari, *21 Lessons for the 21st Century* (Toronto: Penguin Random House Canada, 2018), 318.

6    Harari, *21 Lessons*.

Those of us who enter social work education take what we have learned in the community into the classroom with the aim of supporting both Indigenous and non-Indigenous future social workers in understanding how the current impacts of colonization are at the root of the struggles Indigenous Peoples face today, bringing Indigenous knowledges into their curricula and teaching how to decolonize the system of its biases and racism. Within an Indigenous perspective, what is needed is prevention, rather than the current emphasis on protection, which typically manifests as the apprehension of children. The more prevention, the less protection is needed. I believe this is the future of Indigenous child welfare: supporting families so they can keep children in their communities, helping them to empower themselves, and lessening poverty that is translated into neglect, the major reason why Indigenous children go into care.

Through social work education, we can instill these values and skills in students so they can change Indigenous child welfare through practice, research and policy, creating legislation that reflects Indigenous perspectives and focuses on prevention. Twenty years from now, child welfare for Indigenous families and children will be truly community controlled and culture based, backed with our own Indigenous Family and Child Services Act.

I have also been reading about how emergent curriculum, or what is being referred to as twenty-first century education, is in line with Harari's ideas, and meshes easily with how youth are beginning to collaboratively create content in the virtual world. Stephen Wilmarth observed that "by participating through blogs, wikis, podcasts, video productions on sites such as YouTube, email, text messaging, and shared online photostreams . . . our students are no longer primarily consumers of content . . . they are content creators.".[7] He further proposed that the "messy, nonlinear, highly organic process of learning . . . seems to be at the core of what it takes to be a successful citizen of the 21st century."[8] I love it!

All these principles connect with Indigenous world views about co-operation, collectivity, community and knowing who you are. But just as importantly, institutions of higher education will honour treaties, support sovereignty and establish reciprocal relationships with Indigenous communities and organizations whose territories they are on. There will be more Indigenous people in high-level administrative roles in, for example, student affairs, research and presidencies.

MAKWA: Over time, the necessity to include the United Nations Declaration on the Rights of Indigenous Peoples[9] will be recognized, and it will be implemented first in education. Of course, it will follow article 14, which states, "Indigenous peoples have the right to establish and control their educational systems and institutions providing education in their own languages, in a manner appropriate to

. . . . . . . . . . . . . . . . . .

7     S. Wilmarth, "Five Socio-Technology Trends That Change Everything in Learning and Teaching," in *Curriculum 21: Essential Education for a Changing World*, ed. H.H. Jacobs (Association for Supervision and Curriculum Development, 2010), 82.

8     Wilmarth, "Five Socio-Technology Trends," 95.

9     United Nations, *United Nations Declaration on the Rights of Indigenous Peoples* (2008). https://www.un.org/esa/socdev/unpfii /documents/DRIPS_en.pdf.

their cultural methods of teaching and learning."[10] UNESCO provides both evidence of and solutions to the unbalanced education system not just globally, but also specific to Canada.[11] Sooner rather than later, Indigenous intellectual property will return to Indigenous Peoples, using modern platforms to ensure equal access to Indigenous knowledges in public, private and religious schools. In the future, there will be an Indigenous intellectual hub for global environmental issues that will benefit from Indigenous knowledges pertaining to specific regions in the world. Already, in Toronto, the Toronto District School Board's Urban Indigenous Education Centre serves as a type of Indigenous hub for elementary- and high school-level Indigenous resources[12]; this will continue to flourish in the future and spread to other school boards.

In terms of evaluating Indigenous resources and their implementation into modern-Western curricula, some schools have already created youth-led Indigenous councils, like the High Park Nature Centre's Indigenous Council,[13] to

..................

10     United Nations Educational, Scientific and Cultural Organization (UNESCO), *UN Declaration on the Rights of Indigenous Peoples (UNDRIP) Related to Education and Intergenerational Transmission* (2017). http://www.unesco.org/new/en/indigenous-peoples/education-and-intergenerational-transmission/undrip-ed/.

11     UNESCO (2017).

12     Toronto District School Board, "Indigenous Education" (2014). https://tdsb.on.ca/IndigenousEducation.

13     Parkdale Queen West Community Health Centre, "Niiwin Wendaanimak (Four Winds)" (2020). https://pqwchc.org/programs-services/niiwin-wendaanimak-four-winds/.

ensure accuracy and appropriateness of specific regional Indigenous information like the Wendat. On a much larger scale, there are formal councils of the same makeup that evaluate university- and college-level Indigenous resources and curricula like that of Ryerson University's Aboriginal Education Council.[14] At this level, the council is open to allies who support the bolstering of Indigenous knowledges, resources and intellectual property. In the future, such councils will be an expected piece of education. This will begin the true process of providing the federal government and public, private and religious school boards, an enlightened path of reconciliation with Indigenous communities.

## INDIGENOUS KNOWLEDGES IN EDUCATION:
## THEY WILL LEARN FROM US

CYNDY: Indigenous communities have persevered under processes of colonization and state-sanctioned efforts intended to eradicate them physically, territorially, culturally and linguistically. Despite these acts of violence, Indigenous knowledges have been reclaimed and sustained by Indigenous Peoples in diverse regions around the world. Furthermore, important international recognition has been achieved over the past several decades in the arena of Indigenous rights, which include the right of Indigenous Peoples to protect, maintain and revitalize Indigenous knowledge systems. Indigenous knowledge systems and their manifestations, including

..................

14     Ryerson University, "Aboriginal Education Council." https://www.ryerson.ca/aec/.

traditional ecological knowledge, have served local populations for generations by facilitating thoughtful and deliberate human-environmental interactions.[15] In the future, Indigenous knowledges will lead in what is referred to as environmental sustainability. Thus, within educational institutions, non-Indigenous students will develop an awareness that Indigenous Peoples have been living on our planet for thousands of years and they managed not only to survive but to live on and with the land, learned or developed technologies to help themselves, and cultivated their own values and laws.

The other piece that non-Indigenous students will learn about through their formal education is the history of colonization and how to think critically about its impacts. When they do not learn the history, all they see are the images on the news, and they do not understand what the issues are, why they are happening, or how anti-Indigenous racism plays out. With these understandings, when they hear on the news that Indigenous Peoples are protecting the land and people from pipelines, logging and violence, they will know why and join us.

Twenty years from now we will have much more flexible educational systems, where Indigenous learners feel included, feel that they belong and feel good about who they are as Indigenous people. Education will include Indigenous topics and resources at every grade level and in every subject area.

....................

15      M.N. Tom, E. Sumida-Huaman, and T.L. McCarthy, "Indigenous Knowledges as Vital Contributions to Sustainability," *International Review of Education* 65 (2019), 1–18. https://doi.org/10.1007/s11159-019-09770-9.

Innovative approaches will ensure that students have opportunities to be out in nature to learn about the rivers, the land and the kinship one can acquire by being on and with the land. Elders and Knowledge Holders will do activities with them out on the land. Other educators will help relate Indigenous knowledges to science, math, reading and physical activities. Education will be holistic and integrated. Again, in keeping with Indigenous world views, another advocate of twenty-first century education, has written about the need to educate for the future of the planet, with an emphasis on responsible local and global citizenship, sustainable economics, living within ecological/natural laws and principles, the inclusion of multiple perspectives, and a sense of place.[16]

Teaching in circle, circular classrooms, land-based classes, courses taught in community, more Indigenous professors, and learning from their entire being will be available to all students. Education will then be based on "two-eyed seeing," a concept that Mi'kmaq Elders Albert and Murdena Marshal coined, encouraging learners to see from one eye with Indigenous ways of knowing and from the other eye with mainstream ways of knowing and, importantly, learning to see with both eyes together—for the benefit of all.[17] Indigenous youth will settle for nothing less.

.................

16      J.P. Cloud, "Educating for a Sustainable Future," in *Curriculum 21: Essential Education for a Changing World*, ed. H.H. Jacobs (Association for Supervision and Curriculum Development, 2010), 168–185.

17      C. Bartlett, C., Murdena Marshall and Albert Marshall, "Two-Eyed Seeing and Other Lessons Learned within a Co-learning Journey of Bringing Together Indigenous and Mainstream

MAKWA: The dissolution of Indigenous learning structures was critical for Canada's education system, in which citizens are determined by utility and their ability to feed Canada's economic needs. This is, of course, the worst part of cultural assimilation. However, the medicine wheel structure has become mainstream in some regard, based in apprenticeships, shadowing and philosophical-spiritual guidance from Elders, and influenced by one's individual strengths. Sharla Peltier connects the suppression of Indigenous knowledges and the imposed hostility to Indigenous practical ecological work and theorem as a necessity for capitalist resource extraction in Canada.[18] The idea is that if a relationship to Aki (the earth) can be made, then the responsibility that humanity has to the ecosystem must be taught to youth. This idea will become active practice in Canadian classrooms, with child-first initiatives through relationship-centred, trauma-informed and holistic approaches. This would effectively be the integration of Indigenous principles of child well-being in all stages of a child's life.

In fifty years, Indigenous dispute resolution strategies, as well as region-specific Indigenous knowledges pertaining to trades, social studies, and economy and resource management, will provide infrastructure for

---

Knowledges and Ways of Knowing," *Journal of Environmental Studies and Sciences* 2 (2012) 331–340. https://doi.org/10.1007/s13412-012-0086-8.

18     Sharla Peltier, "Demonstrating Anishinaabe Storywork Circle Pedagogy: Creating Conceptual Space for Ecological Relational Knowledge in the Classroom" (doctoral dissertation, Laurentian University, 2016).

all curricula through the work of Indigenous educators, political leaders and their growing and supportive populations. Youth will always play a crucial role in the future for Indigenous Peoples and the responsibilities outlined by land-based pedagogy. They will do so in classrooms where they will share their ancestral knowledge as it pertains to modern problems. In classroom discussions, their voices will be expanded upon and respected. It is my belief that through direct Indigenous involvement in curriculum, school environments and dispute resolution, more Indigenous youth will obtain the tools they need to become the structural integrity for the future.

## CONCLUSION

CYNDY: Indigenous Peoples have always been resilient and able to adapt to an everchanging world. They have also resisted colonization while never staying static in developing their minds, cultures and knowledges. The strength of our ancestors seven generations back lives in the blood of Indigenous Peoples now, and this will be passed on to the next seven generations into the future. The current generation has begun to consider what truth, reconciliation and healing looks like for Indigenous Peoples. We pass over both our mistakes and our successes to the next generation to learn from. Whether it is twenty years or fifty years into the future, it is this next generation that will bring about what my friend Jeffrey McNeil-Seymour calls "sur-thrivance,"[19] for we will not only survive, we will thrive.

MAKWA: I hope that the current initiatives that I have used to project our future as Indigenous Peoples will be helpful in sparking in all Indigenous youth the will to change things for the better. This will happen by first returning to the medicine to allow Aki to teach Indigenous Peoples as our Ancestors once learned, using old and new knowledge to bring balance to life, for all to walk mino-pimâtisiwin equally. Reconciliation, by facilitating Indigenous autonomy over education and resource management, is an important aspect of this goal. Without recognizing the inherent responsibility to protect the earth, environmental disasters as the aftermath of human intervention are more certain than ever. However, self-determination in Indigenous youth who can access both modern-Western systems and ancestral Indigenous knowledges will provide new ways of managing resources. The appropriate adoption of Indigenous land-based pedagogy, theorems and practices, as well as Indigenous perspectives on child well-being, will ensure a healthy, responsible country, if not a healthy, responsible world. The future of Indigenous Peoples, whether twenty or fifty years in the future, is rooted in the success of Indigenous youth in fields causally related to the land and community.

...................

19    Jeffrey McNeil-Seymour, "Two-Spirit Resistance," in *Whose Land Is It Anyway? A Model for Decolonization*, eds. Peter McFarlane and Nicole Schabus (Federation of Post-Secondary Educators of BC, 2017), 54.

# Future We In-U-Wee

**DR. NORMA DUNNING**
Writer

Are we allowed to dream?
Are we allowed to exceed the parameters of a reality that
     Canada has no interest in?
Are we allowed to be more and better and complete?

Aren't we all supposed to stay in the time of long ago?
The time of standing at a seal breathing hole with a
     harpoon pointing toward small shivers of ice water.
A time of long patience and short lives.
A time of used-to-be.

Used-to-be that Inuit knew their place.
Used-to-be that Inuit only stayed north of sixty and
     not south.
Used-to-be that Inuit never spoke unless there was a
     camera in front of them.
Used-to-be that Inuit kept their faces out of media unless
     they were dead or dying.
Used-to-be that Inuit could go hungry and no one had to
     deal with it.
Used-to-be that Inuit were used to being.

Used to being the people thought of as cute and cuddly.
Used to being the people who were savagely sexy. Fuck a
    skimo and white is not alright.
Used to being the White Ones' doormat.
Used to being the place where all the excrement of
    whiteness laid their visceral leftovers.
Puddles of sperm.
Puddles of snot.

Used to being human spittoons.
Used to being a disk number and not a name.
Used to being moved around, Bedouins of the
    Hudson Bay shoreline.
Used to being human flag poles.

Used to being Canada's biggest afterthought.
An afterthought of every government riddled
    with Alzheimer's.
An afterthought named The Forgotten Ones.

The Forgotten Ones who can still go hungry in 2020.
The Forgotten Ones with twenty-two people crowded into
    one house.
Do not move or you lose your sleeping spot.
The sleeping spot you marked with the stench of you.

The Forgotten Ones are made even more forgettable if
    they dare to move south of sixty.
The land claims made sure of one thing; the thing called
    Don't You Dare.
Don't You Dare try to make a better life for yourself.
Don't You Dare think that your kids deserve a chance.

A chance at a better education.
A chance at being someone. Someone with a university
    degree. Someone who practises law or nursing
    or teaching outside of the invisible borders that
    confine us into a tight little cluster of long ago.

Don't You Dare dream of a future.
Don't You Dare dream that you have somewhere to go
    when there is nowhere to go.
Don't You Dare dream that once you are south people will
    look at you as one of them. You're a freak.

A freak on a city sidewalk, panhandling his life away.
A freak who cannot talk without that accent, anyways eh.
A freak in the limbo of north and south.

South is purgatory.
South is where you get asked if all your kids have the
    same dad.
South is where you cannot apply for northern scholarships.
South is where you get asked if you are Spanish.
South is where you are not really Inuit if you are not eating
    raw meat.
South is where speaking Inuktitut makes you real.
South is where you are asked if you can speak Cantonese.
South is where you get to disappoint people twice in under
    sixty seconds.

South is where your Inuk head glaringly sits on
    StatsCan charts.
South is where StatsCan graphs show you finished
    high school.
South is where StatsCan graphs will make you look like
    a success.
South is where you get a job because you are Inuk.
South is where university degrees tucked inside your back
    pocket do not count.
South is where you get hired because a boss has to fill her
    Indigenous quota.

South is where you get used for your community contacts.
South is where white people harvest your
    Inherent Knowledge.
South is where exploitation of who and what you
    are happens.
South is where the northern Inuit look down their small
    noses at you.
South is where you are neither home nor away.

South is where you become a non-Nunangat Inuk.

A new title.
A new you.
A new anyone else.

If we could live in a world without borders
We would not be different from one another
What if in the future we were not points on a compass
What if the north pole de-magnetized

Allowing all Inuit to de-tox
their thoughts
De-liberately
De-ciding to
De-vote themselves
To one another

What if Inuit stopped letting invisible lines
De-Vide Us
Lines that we cannot see or touch or smell.

What if Future We In-U-Wee fell into each other,
What if Future We In-U-Wee were people without gravity

Nose-diving into love with one another
Twisting and twirling and twitching
Flooding ourselves in the rapture of angelic care
Toward one another

What if Inuit Nunangat, our homeland, was here
        and everywhere?

And Future We In-U-Wee recognized each other
As the Family of The People
No matter where we stand
We are not the remnants of long ago

We are here
We are now
We are the shadows of each other
Wrapped in the cocoon of Creator's hand

A cocoon spun with the fondness of our future selves.

Future We In-U-Wee have food that make their
        bellies burst
Future We In-U-Wee have homes with bedrooms
        for everyone
Future We In-U-Wee have diplomas and degrees dangling
        from their walls
Future We In-U-Wee do not court difference
Future We In-U-Wee
Is today not tomorrow
Future We In-U-Wee
Is the us we are supposed to be

Let us Inuit hold hands
Let us Inuit skip together
Into Future We In-U-Wee

I AM NORMA DUNNING. I wrote this piece out of the love and
hate and disappointment and pride that I have in who Inuit
are. I wrote this piece out of the racism that I have experienced as an Inuk scholar living in the south. I wrote this
piece because I know what it is like to have governments
ignore hunger. Ignore crowded housing. Ignore tuberculo-
sis, a disease absent in the southern areas of Canada but
rampant in the north. Ignore Inuit children who are not
completing high school. We truly are Canada's biggest
afterthought.

        I wrote this piece because of the rejection I feel from
my own. Lateral violence sneaks into our Inuit consciousness and lies there waiting to pounce on one another. I hate
that we buy into colonial measures and markers of each

other. Our ancestors did not do that. Our ancestors welcomed everyone and gave love as their first ingredient to each of us. We have forgotten that.

When I wrote the word, "In-U-Wee" I was thinking of how often the word "Inuit" falls out of non-Inuit mouths in the form of "In-You-It" or "In-O-Wheat" and an assortment of other barnyard sounds. Our own absence as a people in Canada is never articulated properly. As I continued writing "In-U-Wee," it became a word of fun and hope and I could hear that "Wee" echoing inside of my head.

I thought of when my sons were small ones and I would grab their wrists, swing them into the air and say, "Wee Wee Wee," and they'd laugh as their bodies wrote waves splashing into the air. Saying the word "In-U-Wee" sounded like riding on a roller coaster and the fun and excitement and the unknown positive possibilities that lie inside of Inuit future generations. Future fun. Future success. Future us.

Our future is now, not tomorrow. Our future is here. Our future lies within our next breath.

# No Reconciliation in the Absence of Truth and Justice

**ROMEO SAGANASH**
Former Member of Parliament & Jurist

SOME FIFTY YEARS AGO, A YOUNG QUÉBÉCOIS NAMED Jean-Yves Soucy travelled to Eeyou Istchee, deep in the boreal forest in northern Quebec, for a summer job as a fire watchman. He was eighteen. I can imagine his angst because I was sent to a residential school at seven, and the place I walked into in the middle of the night was nothing but strange, alien to my homeland. And so was Jean-Yves's encounter with the James Bay territory, and the Cree. But Ancestors, somehow—as always—determined a certain destiny for Jean-Yves. He stumbled, in a very Columbus-like fashion, upon my late father, William, at the Waswanipi Hudson's Bay post. He asked my dad, William, to guide him during his three-month stint in the otherwise savage, severe environment of the north, and the bush.

Why am I telling this story?

Because it's fitting. Because Jean-Yves asked my dad a Me Tomorrow question.

In a beautifully written book by Jean-Yves titled *Was-wanipi*, published by Boréal after his death, Jean-Yves Soucy recounts William's thoughts about the future of his people, and the resource-extraction industry about to surge upon Eeyou Istchee, his homeland. William's response was striking, and it was not even about himself, or the people, but about the land, waters and animals. Naturally, he was a hunter, fisher and gatherer. He feared for the moose, for example, wondering where they could go without a forest. He feared for the poisoned waters in which the fish would no longer be able to spawn. He predicted—yes, fifty years ago—that the migratory birds would alter their routes in spring and fall. The weather patterns would change drastically, he thought.

It happened. He got it right.

Eeyou Istchee, which is what my people call the Cree territory, has indeed gone through dramatic changes, and rapidly. In fact, the territory and Cree society went through these changes in a matter of a half century, while other societies have gone through similar transformations over centuries. That perspective from the past is crucial to understanding our challenging present and, most obviously, what the future holds for our Nations and peoples. Moving on from here, is it somehow possible that Indigenous Peoples could finally determine their own destiny?

In those times (around 1970), my dad and the Cree People were facing a formidable threat to their land, waters and way of life, as then-premier of Quebec, Robert Bourassa, announced what he called "The Project of the Century." In what was to be known as the James Bay Project, Quebec proposed to dam a number of our major rivers in Eeyou Istchee, thereby flooding a very significant extent of the traditional territory of the Cree and severely impacting their way of life. Although Bourassa and his government knew the Cree have been present in the territory for millennia, they never even bothered to inform the Cree about the plan, let alone ask for their permission. Many meetings and initiatives ensued, including a court case for an interlocutory injunction—thought I'd throw that in there 'cause I like saying "interlocutory injunction"—and a "Stop James Bay" campaign, with campaign material like those T-shirts that read "Don't Panic, Eat Bannock." My favourite recollection of this journey of opposition, however, was that it gave the Cree an occasion to hold their very first general meeting to discuss the proposed project and its far-reaching potential impacts on and consequences for the Cree and their territory. In their genius, our clever leaders of the day submitted to the people a proposed meeting resolution for adoption, which declared forcefully that "only the beavers had the right to build dams" on their territory.

The rest is history, as they say. It was this fierce fight to save our rivers and our way of life, on the ground and before the courts, that finally led to negotiations and the signing of the first modern treaty in Canada: the James Bay and Northern Quebec Agreement. Governments in this country never had, and never will have, a penchant for generosity, especially toward Indigenous Peoples. Quebec and Canada did not wake up one morning and say to us, "Hey, you Crees, we love your beautiful brown eyes, let's sign a modern treaty!" No, it never happens that way, even to this day, and neither, I dare say, will it suddenly happen tomorrow. Suffice to say that the particular history of the James Bay and Northern Quebec Agreement is in itself an exhausting one, especially for those Cree who were tasked with making sure governments honoured and respected their signature. It took a multi-decade struggle and an astounding number of court cases to implement the agreement. But that is another story for another day.

Needless to say, much has happened since 1970 in the Cree world in particular, and with Indigenous lives in general, in this place some call Canada today. The infamous White Paper of 1969, which sought once again to rid Canada of the "Indian Problem," failed notoriously, in the face of staunch opposition by Indigenous Peoples. The Supreme Court of Canada's decision in the Calder case of 1973 led to some meaningful changes in government "land claims" policies. The 1975 James Bay agreement was not only the first modern treaty to be signed in Canada but also the first treaty to be signed that included a province. The 1980s ushered in constitutional promises for Indigenous Peoples but brought along crises as well, if one is to recall the dreary failure of the Meech Lake Accord and, subsequently, the unfortunate defeat of the Charlottetown Accord. I remember these times distinctly because I was bestowed with the honour of being elected to serve as Deputy Grand Chief of the Grand Council of the Crees (Eeyou Istchee) in 1990, shortly after completing law school. I recall how Robert Bourassa stood up in the National Assembly of Quebec to announce the beginning of "James Bay II," a proposed hydro development project on the majestic Great Whale River, once again without informing the Cree People, or consulting with them, or even seeking their permission. Just as he did in the 1970s, just as cavalierly, in true insolent colonialist fashion. I was there as an elected Deputy Grand Chief of the Cree when the so-called Oka Crisis broke out—or, to name it more appropriately, when the Siege of the Kanien'keha:ka began. It was a trying time for the Indigenous people directly targeted, but equally difficult was the backlash against other Indigenous folks in Quebec. The racism we experienced on the streets, in restaurants and bars, at our everyday jobs, became unbearable, oppressive. Nothing like the revolting, inadmissible attack against the Kanien'keha:ka, of course, but still, a sad chapter in Canadian and Indigenous histories. Besides the cop who used the Québécois slur "Kawish" against me at the barricade in Oka, I think to this day the worst was the words of the owner of a renowned restaurant in Old Québec, as he blocked the door of his establishment with his body, telling us we weren't welcome and kindly suggesting that we "go and fetch a fox" for dinner. Relationships were tense, strained, during this time.

Of course, much came after that dramatic moment, from the Delgamuukw case to the establishment of the Royal Commission on Aboriginal Peoples, and the 1995 Quebec Referendum, when my people held their own referendum, four days before Quebec's, to indicate that they weren't going anywhere. Somehow, maybe we thought we were on some path to reconcile our differences in the subsequent years. After all, the Nisga'a Treaty came shortly after, followed by the Marshall decision in the Supreme Court of Canada, and my friend and Cree brother Matthew Coon Come's election as National Chief of the Assembly of First Nations in 2000. The Kelowna Accord came and went, the Indian Residential School Settlement Agreement was finally reached, and the Truth and Reconciliation Commission was tasked with exploring what is certainly one of the most painful and darkest periods—if not *the* most painful and darkest—in Canada's history. As a Residential

School Warrior, having spent a decade behind the walls of one of those institutions, I still sincerely wonder how and why some of my fellow residents are still alive today, given the insufferable physical, sexual, emotional and spiritual violence inflicted on them. The roadmap proposed, the Truth and Reconciliation Commission's 94 Calls to Action, remains largely unheeded by all governments to this day. Former chair and retiring senator Murray Sinclair said in an interview something to the effect that it took Canada 150 years to get us into this mess, and it'll take us another 150 to get out of it. It doesn't have to be that complicated; just some political will and honesty and integrity would take us a long way forward. But there isn't any—thus the unrest throughout the lands of the First Peoples. The Idle No More movement was, among other realities, an Indigenous grassroots movement. I like movements. I was a Member of Parliament by the time Idle No More came to be in 2012, having been elected the previous year, so I sensed at the time that there was something deep and essential on that snowy afternoon in front of the Parliament of Canada that the political class needed to grasp. And I'm not just talking about the non-Indigenous politicians; I'm also referring to the Indigenous politicians, whether chiefs, national or otherwise, band councillors, senators or MPS. Our people feel disenfranchised, and rightly so. The imposed institutions that we've come to accept over time, including the political instruments of the Indian Act, have suspended the capacity, the ability, of our own people to participate in decisions pertaining to their own well-being, their sacred dignity and, most importantly, their very survival and security. Increasingly exasperated, the younger generation is standing up, with full knowledge of who they are, what their fundamental rights mean, and what paths our Nations should now begin to tread. In other words, they claim the right and honour to determine their future, and that should be nothing less than inspiring and compelling for us all. It was for me.

It turns out that in a very trickster-like way, the surprise-loving Ancestors thought it important to strike again, this time making it possible for me to take part in this beautiful Me Tomorrow project.

This long preamble, taken from lessons of my Nookooms when they started a "short story," brings to an end my *avant-propos*; so apropos, though.

ONE EARLY FEBRUARY morning in 2011, I called my friend Jack Layton to tell him I was finally ready to leap into the jungle of federal politics. The federal NDP leader asked what my agenda was for the next day—to which I responded that I had several meetings scheduled. He suggested I postpone them and travel instead to Toronto, to meet him at his house on Huron Street. We had a three-hour discussion. By that time, I thought I had pretty solid experience negotiating with governments and corporations, and I thought I had the upper hand with my friend Jack. I said that I would run in Quebec City, where *everybody* knew me, a riding I thought I could win. He begged to disagree. "Listen," he said, "the global challenges we have are serious, whether it's climate change, protection of the environment, water, Indigenous Peoples, our relations with Indigenous Peoples, resource extraction. *All* of these challenges we find in Northern Quebec, your homeland. You are the best person to represent those peoples. Go back home, Buddy!"

I did.

The ensuing years were ever more telling for me as an Indigenous person, as a Residential School Warrior, as the first Cree from Quebec to obtain a law degree, first Cree from Quebec to be elected to the House of Commons, first Indigenous person to run for leadership of a major political party in Canada—even the first to call the play-by-play of an NHL game in an Indigenous language, in 1987. You can't call a play-by-play in Cree if you don't know your Cree. I did.

First to pronounce "fuck" in the Parliament of Canada? Yes. I meant what I said, and I thank my mother every day for the values she taught me over the years. The story behind that particular day is a long story in itself. Long enough to tell another time.

I spent eight years in a place called the Parliament of Canada, from May 2011 to October 2019. I decided not to seek re-election in the federal election of 2019 strictly because that was the plan; two mandates or else insanity and madness would ensue! However much I had resisted the idea, walking into that institution in 2011 I knew that I would eventually face the challenges any Indigenous person faces when entering not-so-kind places. The hostility is real! Subtle at times, open and direct at others, but very present at every turn. I truly believe that some of those MPs don't even realize they are racist because racism has become so normalized. I was at the Parliament gym in the early days of the Forty-First Parliament's First Session when a Conservative MP approached me while I was working out and asked, with what I believe was politeness according to his standards, "Romeo, when you go hunting, do you guys use rifles?" I knew my time there wasn't going to be a walk in the park! I summoned all of my courage, as I did the night I arrived at La Tuque Indian Residential School at two in the morning, and heard what my late mom had told me the day before on another matter: "Don't complain, you asked for it!"

However challenging some issues may be in a colonial place like the House of Commons, with time, energy, effort and emotion, I did manage to get things done throughout my time in that place. For instance, speaking my Cree language in question period, or for statements or delivering a speech was deemed not in order. In fact, that was my very first inquiry with the clerk of the house, in the very first session. As a jurist, I was told, you should know that the official languages here are French and English. It was a response I couldn't accept—after all, I thought, the right to understand and to be understood is a *fundamental* right. And besides, this language of mine was spoken in this part of the world more than seven thousand years ago. So I fought. It took more than seven years, but it is finally possible for any Indigenous MP to stand up in Parliament and speak in his or her Indigenous language without having to fight for that right.

In keeping with the Truth and Reconciliation Commission's Calls to Action 43 and 44, I also attempted (twice) to get a private member's bill passed to ensure that the laws of Canada are consistent with the United Nations Declaration on the Rights of Indigenous Peoples (UNDRIP). The first attempt was made under the Harper government, so I knew the fate of my bill the day I introduced it, given the Conservatives' staunch opposition to the UNDRIP. I told people at the time my first bill was defeated that I would return with a similar bill should I get re-elected in 2015. I distinctly recall Justin Trudeau standing in front of the Assembly of First Nations Chiefs-in-Assembly in December 2015, less than two months after his election victory, making the solemn promise that his government would introduce legislation to adopt and implement the UNDRIP. True to the popular saying on Parliament Hill, the biggest political challenge in Ottawa is to keep a Liberal promise. So it never happened!

After more than two years and much public pressure, following the 2015 election the Liberal government finally supported Bill C-262, my private member's bill on UNDRIP. Like government bills, private members' bills go through several stages in the House of Commons, including first reading, debate on second reading, and further study by committee if it passes a vote on second reading, before finally being sent back to the House (with or without amendments) for a final vote. Bill C-262 completed all of these stages and was adopted by the Parliament of Canada on May 30, 2018, by a margin of 206 to 79. When the bill was sent to the Senate of Canada for consideration, it was predictably met with resistance and obstruction by the Conservative senators. So, in the end, the five unelected, unaccountable senators managed to filibuster the bill, making it impossible to reach the deadline, with the fast-approaching summer recess, at the end of June 2019. Bill C-262 died on the Order Paper of the Senate, one week after the passing of my mother. In spite of it all, I am proud of that achievement, and grateful for all of the support I was honoured with during the formidable journey of Bill C-262.

One thing I clearly understood, though, the moment I decided to run for office in 2011, was that being a Member of Parliament constitutes an incredible platform. Your space in the public domain increases a thousandfold, and your message thereby has the potential of reaching the entire nation. Across the country, over a year after I left office, people still stop me in the streets, at airports, in restaurants, to gleefully reminisce about the time I told off the prime minister in Parliament. But that was neither the first nor the last time I had a run-in with Justin Trudeau. I wrote him letters, too, with sarcasm at times, as in the opening paragraph of this one:

Dear Prime Minister,

It's been a while since my past letter, I'm sorry about that. We don't talk like we used to; it's been tense at work. We've both said some things we probably both regret. You with your promises to Indigenous people, promises that you won't live up to, and me with some strong language in the House of Commons: but I really meant what I said.

And there was this other time when the prime minister truly triggered me to the point where I had to reach deep to find the best coping mechanism we possess as Indigenous folks: humour.

Like the majority of non-Indigenous politicians in the country, whether at the municipal, provincial or federal level, Trudeau always thinks he knows what's best for us. In two consecutive town hall appearances in 2017, he said, "I've spoken with a number of chiefs who said, 'You know, we need a youth centre . . . You know, we need TVs and lounges and sofas so they can hang around.' And when a chief says that to me, I pretty much know they haven't actually talked to their young people." And he continued, "because most of the young people I've talked to want a place to store their canoes and paddles so they can connect back out on the land." Patronizing, yes indeed—comments that of course I could not allow to remain unanswered, given my position as a member sitting across the aisle from the prime minister. The letter was front-page news, so reproducing it here is definitely in order:

February 6, 2017

Subject: National Canoe and Paddle Program

Mr. Trudeau,

Your government has yet to invest the money required under legal obligations to end the racial discrimination of First Nations youth. However, as an Indigenous person I understand if there may not be enough money for the federal government to meet its legal and moral obligations to our children. You can trust me that I truly understand why the Canadian government may not be able to respect our rights. Over the course of the history of Canada, First Nations children have received more than our fair share so it is probably time for our youth to wait a turn. That is why, if you must make a choice in the upcoming budget, I am writing to you today to express my desire for a National Canoe and Paddle Program.

As a Cree man, not only was I born on the shores of a lake, but I have spent much of my life navigating waters. However, I want you to know that it wasn't until your recent comments that I fully understood the importance of having storage for our canoes and paddles. In fact, I am ashamed for my people that we haven't been listening to our youth in the way you have. But, it did make me thankful that the Prime Minister of this great country can continue to enlighten my peoples when he stated:

> *"I've spoken with a number of chiefs who said, 'You know, we need a youth centre . . . You know, we need TVs and lounges and sofas so they can hang around.' And when a chief says that to me, I pretty much know they haven't actually talked to their young people because most of the young people I've talked to want a place to store their canoes and paddles so they can connect back out on the land and a place with internet access so they can do their homework."*
> —*Prime Minister Trudeau, 2017*

It is truly an honour for the first time in the history of Canada to have a Prime Minister as the Minister of Youth so plugged into our kids. As Prime Minister, you wrote to every member of Cabinet affirming that your relationship with Indigenous Peoples is the most important one, so who am I to argue with your recent comments that you know what is best for Indigenous youth facing so many critical issues including a suicide epidemic.

That is why I believe a National Canoe and Paddle Program is absolutely critical to Indigenous youth. I believe this is also why the Truth and Reconciliation Commission made this national program the secret 95th Call to Action.

Further, I am heartened and encouraged to see that your government is truly embracing the spirit of the UN Declaration Including Article 25, which reads,

*Indigenous peoples have the right to maintain and strengthen their distinctive spiritual relationship with their traditionally owned or otherwise occupied and used lands, territories, waters and coastal seas and other resources and to uphold their responsibilities to future generations in this regard.*

It is time for the federal government to help First Nations maintain our very important spiritual connection with the water. This is a connection that your government further embraces through your approval of projects like Site-C, Kinder Morgan, and the Muskrat Falls Dam. Once the canoe and paddle storage system is in place, I will personally paddle across the country to tell First Nations concerned with the impacts of these projects, not to worry because with these urgently needed budget investment for canoe storage depots our connection to the lands and waters is maintained.

While I am not the Prime Minister whose primary relationship is with Indigenous Peoples, I would like to make you aware of the fact that I founded the Cree Nation Youth Council in 1985. I feel this should provide the tiniest of assurances that I can speak from experience and expertise when I say that the biggest issue facing Indigenous youth for the last 150 years has been the lack of sheds to store our canoes. I myself have often lamented the lack of space on

Parliament Hill to store my canoe and paddle. I commend your vision, Prime Minister, and look forward to your government addressing this immediate crisis in the upcoming budget.

Sincerely,
Romeo Saganash

The headline in the *National Post* read, "Trudeau was always a joke to the right; he should worry now the left's joined in the laughter," with the subheading, "The right has long lampooned Trudeau for being too stupid, too callow, too entitled to be a successful prime minister. But Saganash's attack is much more devastating."[1]

It goes without saying that Mr. Trudeau never bothered to respond to my letter, nor even cared to acknowledge receipt of it. I regret to inform Indigenous youth that the national canoe and paddle program I suggested has not come to be, and I very much doubt Justin will deliver on this promise, ever.

I often wonder what my legacy will be for those who will follow. I am too humble to suggest anything. But I do regret that I have to conclude, after what I've observed over the last forty years of attempting to fix the mess we are in, left behind by successive Liberal and Conservative governments at the federal level, that the mess will most certainly

....................

1    John Ivison, "Trudeau Was Always a Joke to the Right; He Should Worry Now the Left's Joined in the Laughter" (*National Post*, February 10, 2017). https://nationalpost.com/news/politics/john -ivison-trudeau-was-always-a-joke-to-the-right-he-should-worry -now-the-lefts-joined-in-the-laughter.

continue for decades to come. Politics over the last century and a half have been too willfully stubborn—and difficult, to say the least—to allow for any genuine attempt at change, real change! The political and legal resistance of governments against respecting the fundamental rights of the world's 400 million Indigenous people in more than seventy countries is no different than in this country called Canada. And yet solutions exist, and have been proposed over the years by commissions and individuals. To no avail. We can hardly even call the development and advancement of the recognition of Indigenous Rights incremental, we are moving at such a snail's pace. In this context, though, I prefer the expression and image used in Quebec: "C'est comme la mélasse au mois de janvier." (It's like molasses in January!) Since their election in 2015, Prime Minister Trudeau and his ministers have been exceptionally effective in saying one thing to Indigenous people and actually doing the exact opposite in their actions and practices. Even the Canadian Human Rights Tribunal noted this fact with obvious disappointment. My good friend and brother Payam Akhavan, in his book *In Search of a Better World*, reveals quite pointedly that "the problem with the world is not a shortage of brilliant theories or feel-good slogans. The problem is that we confuse proliferation of progressive terminology with profound empathy and purposeful engagement. We say the right things, but we fail to act on them because we want to feel virtuous without paying a price."[2] Hear reconciliation here! Hear that the most important relationship

..................

2      Payam Akhavan, *In Search of a Better World: A Human Rights Odyssey*, CBC Massey Lectures (Toronto: House of Anansi Press, 2017).

with Indigenous Peoples for Justin is in words here, in the absence of action. There can't be any reconciliation with Indigenous Peoples in the absence of action, in the absence of justice.

MY FATHER PASSED on to the Spirit World fifty years or so ago. I was privileged to have shared even a mere seven years with him before I was kidnapped and sent to residential school. He taught me many values, including kindness, humility and the pursuit of what was always his fundamental purpose: to provide for the family, for the community, for the Nation, for the people. Over the last forty years, including eight of them as a legislator, I have strived to match his goals and efforts in my own way. I have attempted in good conscience to achieve what I thought was the right thing to do.

My father predicted in 1971 what we would face as predicaments and challenges in 2021. I long for his presence today, wishing he would tell me at this moment that all will be okay, that my pessimism is unwarranted, that our kids, my kids and grandchildren, will be all right. But he isn't here now, and neither is my mom. Unless the political and legal stubbornness miraculously ceases in favour of an attitude of respect for the constitutional and international human rights of Indigenous Peoples, I'm afraid my time and efforts in the last forty years will have been insufficient to improve the situation by 2071.

But we are still here. We will still be here later, too. I know the resilience of our people. I take comfort in the fact that the younger, up-and-coming leadership will be better at determining the Indigenous narrative from here on. It's about the survival, dignity, the well-being and security of Indigenous Peoples.

That's what we've been fighting for over the last 529 years, since 1492.

Deskaheh, of the Iroquois League, attempted to crash the Assembly of the League of Nations (the predecessor to the United Nations) in Geneva in 1923, to plead for the recognition and sovereignty of the six Nations he represented. The Assembly refused to hear Deskaheh's plea, and shut its doors on him. Shortly after, in his final speech, just prior to his passing, it is said that he exhorted his people to continue to fight for Iroquois rights "just as the whiteman defends his rights."

I come from a long line of great hunters, trappers, fishers and gatherers. Like the majority of young people back then, I aspired to be like my dad, the great canoe builder and snowshoe maker, the ultimate provider for the family and community. That hope, of course, was shattered by Ottawa, which had other plans for me and my generation. I would have chosen writing or photography, or become a wine bar owner; I definitely wouldn't have chosen politics. I'm not even certain today about how I fared on that merciless journey, but I take comfort in the fact that none of my children have chosen the path I unintentionally stumbled upon—at least not yet!

APPARENTLY A PRESS conference has been called for tomorrow by the minister of Indigenous–Crown Relations and the attorney general of Canada. My informants tell me it is a major break from the traditional practice of the federal government in relation to Indigenous Peoples and their rights. For the first time in the history of the country now called Canada, the attorney general will have an obligation to make sure, before introducing any legislation, that it is consistent with the United Nations Declaration on the Rights of Indigenous Peoples, as well as section 35 of the Canadian Constitution. Under article 4.1(1) of the Department of Justice Act, the minister of justice already has the obligation to verify the conformity of legislation with the Charter of Rights and Freedoms, but no obligation exists with respect to Indigenous Rights and treaty rights. That's about to change, whispers my faithful informant and journalist friend on what is now the Penoshoway Hill—formerly known as Parliament Hill—recognizing the Anishinaabe family that have lived, hunted, fished and gathered there for millennia. This measure would also apply to all decisions of the Cabinet and the government in regard to land and resource development.

As I listen to the ministers the next day, one phrase in particular strikes me. The minister of justice says for the first time in the history of Canada, "We believe in justice for Indigenous people in this country and we are therefore announcing today that we are putting in place measures to avoid future conflicts before the courts with the present and future generations of Indigenous people. We have lost most of our cases at the Supreme Court in the past, and we believe that the billion dollars we spend fighting Indigenous people in the courts every year would be more wisely spent on houses and clean drinking water, for instance." I call Minister of Justice Buffalo Jump the next day to express my gratitude, and tell him that his government's monumental decision will allow my children to invest their time in better, greater and more fulfilling endeavours, like music, theatre and writing.

The minister begins to respond with soothing prose about how he finally understands the Indigenous soul and spirit—and just as he is beginning to tear up, my cellular phone, which I left in the living room, starts to ring and snatches me out of my dream. As I turn off the cell phone, I wish the dream were a premonitory one.

If this were the course Canada embarked on today, tomorrow—maybe in fifty years—our children and grand-children would not be suffering the kind of crap we have had to endure over the last 250 years, even with the prom-ise of the Royal Proclamation that as Nations, we would not be "molested" or "disturbed" by the settlers on our own lands. But once the settlers realized that they did not need us anymore, or considered Indigenous people as hindering their "progress" toward the colonization and disposses-sion of Indigenous lands, territories and resources, the opposite happened.

As justification for not doing anything meaningful to fix the troubled and often violent relations between governments and Indigenous Peoples, I am frequently told that I must appreciate how difficult these constitutional and political matters are, and how it will therefore take an eternity to resolve them.

For so many years and by commission after com-mission, solutions have been proposed, and yet we are left to wonder why these relations between us continue to be perpetually strained. How about a simple proposition, then? How about we start with something as basic and fundamental as the value of respect? It is telling that the United Nations thought it important to emphasize this principle from the outset in the United Nations Declaration on the Rights of Indigenous Peoples. Indeed, the second paragraph of the preamble to this universal international human rights instrument affirms that "indigenous peoples are equal to all other peoples, while recognizing the right of all peoples to be different, to consider themselves different, and *to be respected as such*" (emphasis mine).

If we are sincere and truthful about this country's people's desire to walk the path of reconciliation together, then that journey must be undertaken now. No more excuses. Kill the weasels in those politicians today! A great constitutional reset is overdue, and the need to start over has now become utterly imperative. That is what I believe the Truth and Reconciliation Commission is imploring us to do in its Call to Action 45:

> We call upon the Government of Canada, on behalf of all Canadians, to jointly develop with Aboriginal peoples a Royal Proclamation of Reconciliation to be issued by the Crown. The proclamation would build on the Royal Proclamation of 1763 and the Treaty of Niagara of 1764, and reaffirm the nation-to-nation relationship between Aboriginal peoples and the Crown.[3]

The enumeration of commitments that would accompany this foundational constitutional initiative will have far-reaching implications for both Indigenous people and

3    Truth and Reconciliation Commission of Canada, *Truth and Reconciliation Commission of Canada: Calls to Action* (Winnipeg, MB: TRC, 2015), 4. http://trc.ca/assets/pdf/Calls_to_Action_English2.pdf.

Canadians. It seems a simple place to start, but this new adventure has the potential to take us to that elusive moment in our lives when we realize that the unexpected "second chance" has come—if only fleetingly!

The challenge Canadians face is simply to truthfully reflect on what really made this country possible today, and at what expense the Canadian dream was possible; to think about what was destroyed, and about those who perished along with the destruction of lands, systems, children, ways of life, cultures and traditions. Equally crucial is the need to revisit and re-embrace the teachings of the Ancestors, collectively, in this country—all of us. This seems even more relevant today as we witness seriously tumultuous times around the world. *Love* should be honoured always, *respect* should be upheld unconditionally, *courage* should not be a response to fear but a bold empathy for others. *Honesty* must become the underlying principle of our relations, lessons of our mutual past the national trait of our collective *wisdom*, *humility* our constitutional ethos, and *truth* our path henceforth.

Indeed, I do not fail to grasp the beauty in a little girl, born of settler parents from Western Canada, greeting my grandchild Edouard in Cree: "Watchiya Nawidjawagan!" (Hello, my friend!). We are compelled to do all this today, so my grandchildren will be able to experience their right to joy tomorrow, along with the right to be different, and to be respected as such.

# In the Blink of an Eye

**AUTUMN PELTIER**
Age 17, Activist & Water Rights Advocate

A S I SIT HERE LOOKING OUT MY OFFICE WINDOW, watching a thunderstorm roll in, a memory of me at sixteen crosses my mind. It was the year COVID-19 hit our world, and everything just stopped. I remember being so busy with water activism and advocating for the rights of Indigenous people. And I thought, wow, most kids want to get their driver's licence and buy a car, but I was focused on getting As and applying for university. It was the only thing I could think about. I would remember my Mishoomis (grandfather), an educator, always stressing learning land-based ways, living off the land and staying away from institutional learning. Then I would panic because I knew that we in my generation, Gen Z, would be the ones who would lose it all for our culture. I tried not to think of this, but it was always in the back of my mind. I remember my late Aunt Josephine always saying, "Never stop the work you're doing, don't let anyone stop you, keep learning and keep loving the water." I would often hear in my mind the voices of my Elders when I saw things not going right. But I also knew that to survive in this world I needed the white man's education, even though it wasn't our way.

I'm forty-six years old now. The storm arrives and it is pouring rain. I glance at the wall and see many certificates and photos, and a few degrees. I see the photos of my family on my desk, and the Indigenous art throughout the room. There is soft drumming in the background. I remember how hard the struggle was to get to where I am now. I had the opportunity to experience things that not many Indigenous youth get to experience. My path was set from the age of eight. I don't know what happened that day, but when I learned that kids my age and younger couldn't drink their water, the fire inside me bellowed like a roaring forest fire. That is when this journey began. I had my eyes on making sure that our voices would be heard and that the future of water, the future of our Indigenous ways, would survive all this human-made destruction.

I stare at a photo on my desk of my eldest child's post-secondary graduation. I remember being where she was. I also remember the voices of my Elders speaking to me, and hearing their cries for help: "Who will carry on the work?" That was a lot of pressure for a teenager. Attending meetings with Elders, chiefs and very educated people. Sometimes I would think, what the heck am I doing here? Sometimes while listening and learning, the way I heard things would not be what they were saying. But would they even see it my way? Our way as teens was very simple. Most times I though people were looking at me like I had another head growing out of my body or I was another colour. Often I thought that adults were just afraid to talk to us teens, because we could turn on a dime, or go from zero to sixty in seconds, sort of like in *The Exorcist*, with our heads spinning a few times. At times I felt like that was our advantage, and it was a time when our voices were very strong. Some days I really had to practise patience and not say things; I had to choose my battles. So today I can really relate to my daughter and where she is at, what she stands for. All it took was for my own mother to listen to and hear me. Not only that, but she believed in me. So I've made sure to always listen to my kids. I didn't want karma to come looking for me.

Back to the voices of our Elders. There was a time when I just wanted to be a teen and do teen things. I wanted to give my mom a headache, I wanted to be destructive. But for some reason those voices always stopped me. As a child I had said to myself, "One day I'm going to be an Elder, and then one day I will be an Ancestor." But when I lost my grandmother, things really began to shift within me. I thought, "Who is going to do these ceremonies when my mom is gone and when my grandfather is gone? What will I have to leave behind to the ones coming behind me, what kind of grandmother will I be?" That was when I began paying more attention and really watching.

My mother raised us girls to know our ways so we could carry things on when she was gone. She spent many years travelling to ceremonies, visiting Elders, seeing healers and meeting knowledge keepers along the way. Her goal was to pass on the teachings so they would not be lost, so we could still be who we are, stand up for our rights, use our voices, protect the lands, protect the waters and protect the treaties. My two sisters and I finally got what she was trying to do. Many years she sacrificed for us; everything she did was for us, and she showed us what it is to be an Anishinaabe woman. On that day when I was eight years old, she told me what it meant to be born a woman, and as an Anishinaabe-Kwe.

It was a huge responsibility that we carried. She told me right from the creation story how I picked my parents and how my path was already made by the Creator. She told me how for nine months I lived in water, and how she kept her waters calm because she didn't want to pass on intergenerational trauma. She told me how we got our first water teaching when we were in her waters. She told me how life can't be made without water, as fetuses need water for development and survival. It is also where we learn unconditional love. And when the water breaks, like snow melting in the spring, new life comes. She told me as Anishinaabe-Kwe it is our role to nurture and teach the young girls. I remember her telling me of the importance of the berry fast and what it meant. Then that day came and I had to do mine. So many lessons were learned, but it wasn't like reading a book, or Googling a ceremony—it was hands-on and it was our way of life. Even though we lived in mainstream society, my mother always managed to keep the Anishinaabe way in our lives. She always used to say, "You can take an Indian off the Rez, but you can't take the Rez out of the Indian!" Even in the big fancy city known as the Nation's Capital, my mother wore her long, long hair in braids. She wore beaded earrings and native T-shirts. Some days she wore ribbon skirts. She would say, "It's who I am, and I'm proud of it!" I always liked how we would go shopping and she would say, "This would look deadly with my ribbon skirt." Sometimes she would find the most Indigenous things in the oddest places, and she'd say, "I knew I would find one of these someday!"

We can learn many things from our mothers if we just take the time to listen and reflect. Every day was an opportunity to learn something new or old, or to try again. I've spent my years making sure I had something to offer my grandchildren. Just like I said in my speeches, many moons ago, as a youth activist.

LET ME SHARE with you my fondest memory of travelling with my mother.

I was thirteen, and it was our first time flying across the ocean in a plane. We were on our way to Stockholm. I remember my mom saying that she made sure to pay the cell phone bill so we could use our data, and that she'd made sure to pay for the foreign data package. Then she said she put all her belief in Asemaa and Google Maps.

So here we are, landing in a foreign country. We don't speak the language and she says we have to look like we fit in. LOL. She never fits in anywhere we go, I think to myself. No matter where we go, someone always says *Hola* to her, assuming she is Latina. She is always like a walking Waldo: in a crowd of thousands, yep, you can find her. Most Indigenous one around, minus the feathers—though I know she would wear those too if she wanted to. Anyway, here we are, trying to read the signs in Swedish. She says, "There's free Wi-Fi here. I'm going to use my Google Maps." I ask, "Who's meeting us, and where do we go?" She looks at me and says, "Don't worry, I have the address. If no one is waiting for us, we will find our way."

She opens her phone and types in the address. Then she says, "The lady said not to take a cab, as they will know we are visitors and rip us off." Then, "We are not far away from the train station." So she sets Google Maps for walking directions—this crazy woman with a huge suitcase, like she plans to live in Stockholm for a month. The streets are cobbled, and all you can hear is "click, click, click, click" as we walk, pulling our suitcases. Not to mention that we are now lugging them up a steep street. She says calmly, "It's not far, we're almost there." Meanwhile we've been walking for twenty minutes. Here we are, thousands of miles away from home, we know no one, and nobody speaks English.

As we are walking, I observe that there is no gum, no garbage and no cigarette butts on the ground. I say, "Mom, it's so clean here." She replies, "They probably knew the clean water advocate would be walking down this street and had it all cleaned before you walked here." On every corner there are recycling bins and waste containers. Also water fountains where you can fill your reusable containers. People appear very friendly, and everyone's clothing looks like it's from H&M or Cabela's. We notice many blond and very tall people. The women are especially tall. My mom says, "Make sure not to smile at the tall blond men. That's what happened to Pocahontas. Next thing you know, 'John Smith' took her to the old world, and we know how that story ended."

Finally, as we turn a corner, she says, "Here it is, we made it." We arrive at what looks to me like an IKEA store. We walk in and the atmosphere is very different. You can just feel that we are somewhere different. When we get to our room it's like walking into an IKEA showroom. Everything feels like a display. But it's very nice, modern with a retro feel and fancy fabric patterns. It feels good to have made it this far, and we start to let family and leadership know we've arrived safely. Thank goodness for free Wi-Fi around the world. Later my mom says, "I feel like I am in a scene from the movie *American Werewolf in London*, or *Interview with a Vampire*." I look at her and she says, "Close the curtains—I don't want the werewolves or vampires to find us." Well, thanks a lot for creeping me out. But it really does look that way once I've Googled to see what she's talking about.

The food is different too. They sure eat a lot of cheese and chocolate in Sweden. The next morning, the breakfast counter has various types of sandwich meat, cheeses, fruits and breads. But my mom says, "Where's the porridge or cream of wheat?" She finds it and suddenly she's happy in her own world, enjoying breakfast. Also there's no plastic in this city. They also give us reusable glass bottles with lids. Everyone has their own reusable containers. I thought this was very cool. We sure can learn a lot from how they recycle, reuse and reduce.

IT WAS ALWAYS an adventure travelling with my mom, and to be honest, she always made things fun, even when I didn't feel like doing half the things she got me to do. She always made it an adventure. She would say, "What would Auntie-Jo want to see, or what would Nana do, if they could be with us right now?" So the adventures we went on for my clean water work were always fun, with funny and unexpected occurrences.

In January 2020, for example, just before the COVID-19 pandemic began, we attended the World Economic Forum in Davos, Switzerland. On one of the forum days, we notice that everyone has disappeared. My mom says, "Everyone went into the main hall, where we saw Donald Trump speak." So we go to the door and I peek in. My mom whispers, "Do you want to go in and listen to the speaker?" I say,

"No, it's just some older fellow who I don't know." (It turned out that the speaker just happened to be Charles, Prince of Wales.) "Okay," she says, "let's wander around and wait over this way and eat these fancy appetizers." She jokes about wishing she had a ziplock container so she could take some for snacks later.

So we're standing outside of this hall, munching on fancy snacks. We hear heels walking quickly toward us. My mom looks up and says, "Hey, Autumn, look! It's Ivanka Trump." I look up and I say no, that's not her. Then a woman stops her and says "Why, hello there, Ivanka." While they talk about the day and the women's powder room, my mom is fumbling to try and get a quick photo of Ivanka, at the same time as she's trying to wipe crumbs off her face. So funny: these two little Indigenous women standing off to the side, watching all the happenings like two flower pots in a window.

Later, we decide to go for a walk and explore Davos in the couple of hours before my panel with other Indigenous youth from around the world. As we are walking, she says, "I think we are being followed." We pick up the pace, and then she says, "Let's go into one of these venues and pretend we are participants." We do our best to blend in, and the people following us walk on by. After a few minutes, we leave. My mom sees a pizza shop and says, "Let's dip in there and grab some water or juice." As we go in, we see the people following us see us through the window. "Quick, let's order a slice of pizza," my mom says. "That way, we are sitting here and maybe they will go away." After we eat our pizza, we go outside—and they are there, waiting. It turns out that all this time this group of officials had just wanted a photo with me, but they didn't speak English. They were diplomats from China—I think they said one of them was the prime minister of China.

Another time, I was invited to do a modelling contract with a well-known sports retailer, which required us to fly to Los Angeles. Talk about being somewhere in the blink of an eye. It all happened so fast. One day we are being picked up in a fancy car with a driver, then we are on a plane landing in Boston, and then we're off to Los Angeles. I didn't know it at the time, but my mom had no money, and here we were on a plane heading to the USA. Luckily, the organization took really good care of us. We ate on the plane, we didn't have to pay for the taxi, we didn't even have to carry our bags. The airport in Los Angeles reminded me of LaGuardia, in New York City. Wow, talk about a busy place! So many people rushing here and there, so many people in a big hurry. The funny thing was that most people we interacted with spoke Spanish to my mom. She was almost annoyed, but then she started agreeing and saying thank you in Spanish. (I had no idea she could do that, but that's another funny story in itself.) Our chauffeur arrived with a sign on an iPad that read "Peltier," and off we went.

We didn't stop in Los Angeles. I asked my mom where we were going, and she said, "I don't know—we just got in the car that had our names on it." I whispered, "Mom, so we got into a car with a stranger who's driving us to who knows where and no one knows where we are?" She replied, "Someone knows we are in this car, going somewhere." Going somewhere very calmly, as she gently puts tobacco outside the window. We drive about two hours out of Los Angeles. We finally arrive at this beautiful hotel in a California town called Santa Clarita. She says, "Great, we are now in a town where there's zombies. Hopefully we won't end up as part of someone's diet."

The next day, another car is awaiting us. So again we get in and are driven for two hours. The roads are getting smaller, and we are now in the California desert. And there, in the middle of the desert, is this amazing photo set. Apparently movies have been filmed there. It is dusty and hot, and there are warnings about rattlesnakes. It is fun getting my hair and makeup done, checking out the wardrobe with amazing people.

After eight hours of trying on and changing clothes, it was time to go. Then, after eight hours of shooting, it was back to the airport. And just like that, within a twenty-four-hour period, we were back home in Ontario. That is what I call a whirlwind experience. In the water work adventures, anything can happen.

SO AS I sit here in my office, thirty years later, I look at my wall and see the degrees, diplomas, certificates and awards. They read, Combined Honours Bachelor of Arts in Political Science and Indigenous Studies, Carleton University; Master of Science in Community Health, and Master of Environmental Science, University of Toronto; Juris Doctor, Osgoode Hall Law School; and Doctor of Philosophy, Yale University. I work for Indigenous Peoples. I sit on various Indigenous committees at the United Nations. And I continue to support charities that will help Indigenous youth and girls learn land-based teachings. There are land-based centres all over North America to connect with ceremony and connect with Elders, their language and their culture. I also sponsor many programs to help youth access funding for sports, recreation and education. Communities are working together on state-of-the-art water treatment plants, and many green and solar projects that are less harmful to the earth.

Thinking back to when I first began this journey, I was upset about the fact that there were children younger than me who never even knew what clean, running water was. Children in Canada, a very resource-wealthy country, also known as a richer country—where Indigenous Peoples live in Third-World conditions. I had never realized it myself, and I learned that many Canadians had no idea my people lived this way. Yes, I heard complaints about how my people had certain things taken care of by the government, such as health care and education, and didn't have to pay taxes. I heard how our people were hated and talked about for being homeless or drunks or addicts. Little did they know my people were suffering from the intergenerational impacts of genocide by the Canadian government and its Indian residential schools. My people were wounded, abused and treated like animals. Sort of hard to live your life after all of that.

All I wanted was for the Indigenous Peoples in Canada to have clean drinking water. Some communities had waited over twenty years to have the federal government answer their pleas. No child should have to wait for clean water. So that is when I started to use my voice to create awareness and help where I could. So for thirty years I advocated and used my voice. Nothing is perfect and I do what I can for the communities. Even after thirty years, we are still fighting for clean water. Aunt Josephine began her work in 2003, and here we are in 2051, still fighting for clean water. It has made me feel discouraged many times. It has made me think, why did I stay on this path? What would

I be doing, or what would I have become, if I hadn't taken this path? Many times I wanted to quit, but I kept hearing my aunt's voice: "Don't stop the work, don't let anyone stop you and keep loving the water."

Today, I have dedicated all of my education and my work to ensuring that we have clean drinking water and that we keep our Great Lakes safe from harm. I managed to get the Great Lakes protected from profiteering and from destruction of the natural environment. Human rights for water. It took years, but we managed together to stand up for our waters. The federal government has still never cleared up the boil water advisories in Indigenous communities, but we have worked together to create more policies and we've worked together on solutions. New policies, new regulations and new technology have been introduced to the communities.

My work has inspired excellent networking sponsors that have been generous suppliers and contributors to our cause. The policies we've created have ensured that no community will ever wait more than one to four years for water treatment support. We have established working groups and councils just for monitoring the water issues on Indigenous lands. There are scholarships and bursaries that youth can apply for to continue their work for the environment. There are now educational curriculums based on connection to the land and land-based knowledge for Indigenous youth. We did this to help the youth reclaim their culture at a time when we have lost many Elders and teachers. I recall saying I hope I won't be seventy-five years old and still doing this advocacy because nothing has been done. With all my work locally and internationally, I managed to gain the connections I needed to help advocate for

Indigenous people. The framework I have established has gained recognition among various other Indigenous groups around the world. Our fight is not over. I've always thought how sad it is that First Peoples have to fight for their rights, always and in every way. My whole life has revolved around helping Indigenous Peoples and supporting their human rights in all aspects, as everything is connected. My goal and my hope is that the ones coming behind me will continue our fight for clean water, as we are coming to a time when our waters are the precious resource that the world is fighting over.

Everything I have done seemed to happen in the blink of an eye. My path was set for me all in one day. I thank my late Great-Aunt Josephine Mandamin, my late grandmother Marita Mandamin-Peltier and my mother for getting me on the path to never forgetting who we are, and to working for the environment. For thirty-eight years I have done this work, and I feel I can work for another thirty years before I retire as a spirit in this physical experience. My little mother is now seventy-six years old. She is still doing what she loves—ceremonies, teachings and sharing knowledge where she can. She is my number one supporter and she has always helped me succeed. Her goal was to make sure her daughters carried on the work of our aunt, and her own work. If trauma can be passed down through the generations, so can teaching and healing. I only hope we can continue to pursue their wishes and dreams, as they have sacrificed for us.

Listen to your Elders and take the time to listen to the kids. Take that five minutes to hear what children have to say, as you never know who you are listening to and where their path will take them. On that day when I was eight years old, my mom listened to me and asked me what I wanted to do. She empowered me. That is why we honour our mothers, and honour the waters we come from, because without water none of us would be here.

When the Ancestors are calling and your spirit hears their calls, no matter what age you are, never ignore it. Follow your spirit. Trust your spirit and let it guide you. You never know where you will end up, what you will see, who you will meet, what you will learn. The experiences you will have when you trust your spirit and creator are endless.

Miigwech from Mskwaa-Giiso-Kwe, Migizi Ndodem Wiikwemkoong Ndoonjii (Autumn Peltier).

# A'tukwewinu'k (storytellers)[1]

**SHALAN JOUDRY**
Storyteller, Poet, Playwright & Ecologist

"JUST THINK," HE SAYS TO THE GROUP, "SEVEN GENERA-tions ago someone was sitting here planning for your existence." We are circled about a fire in a modern wi'kuom. Yes, the covering is made of canvas, making it a "non-traditional" wi'kuom, although *wi'kuom* in our L'nu (Mi'kmaw) language simply means dwelling where we live. In today's time, we only sit there when we are teaching or retreating, a choice to be under the folds and poles of this home.

Frank and i are sharing stories the old way, around a fire, dirt under our feet. Sometimes i take off my shoes. It doesn't seem right to have hiking boots on inside the wi'kuom. I move the dry dirt with my foot as he speaks. Outside of the wi'kuom is a young mixed forest, here in the back

..................

1    This essay is inspired by the teachings of the many oral storytellers i have known around many fires, including my parents and my partner, as well as Elder writer-storytellers like Lee Maracle and Thomas King. Wela'lioq.

section of the reserve. Frank built a few small cabins and a short trail as a rustic retreat for people to come and "defrag," he calls it. I have heard this story before. After another hour it will be my turn to share with the visitors. For now, i lose myself in thought, entranced by the fire and Frank's voice.

When i sit by the fire or water, i let my mind wander to the past, to the present challenges and to the future. Some days it feels as though we are already in the slow shifting of our demise. I recognize that many of our Indigenous ancestors already experienced the end of their world as they knew it. We must, as humans, find our own vision forward so that we have something to steady us each morning.

To help me vision, i imagine how i hope today would have been had European colonization happened differently, had it taken place as a partnership in our territories rather than as an attempt at genocide and assimilation. What would it look like if we had co-created Canada between Indigenous nations of northern Turtle Island and the Europeans who were fleeing their own lands? Some of the things i focus on are how to educate our children, how to balance with the natural world and how to keep oral story alive.

Sitting there with the fire, i visualize the generations yet to be born and the lives they will lead.

Like all fields of art, there will be so much diversity in Indigenous theatre and storytelling that we will not know what or how to categorize "Indigenous." One of the forms that i can envision is the future of the old style of Indigenous oral storytelling. I can imagine that in the future there's going to be even more far-reaching technologies that i can't fathom right now. There will be so many forms of storytelling and theatre that i can't even dream up the multitude of possibilities.

What i can see ahead is the constant weaving and reshaping of the old into the new. As an ecologist and someone fascinated with the traits in us that are intrinsic or natural, i believe that the old cultural traditions—the ones that are healthy for all—will in fact persist. As much as i am inspired by modern art forms, i truly believe that some very basic teachings of the land will never completely go out of style.

Some of my dreams are inspired by the notion that for the past thirteen thousand years of humans living in Mi'kma'ki, people have known the land and created stories of the land and each other in order to survive. Our L'nu ancestors embodied and carried those stories from one generation to the next for so long, updating them at each necessary step. These stories of the land and history have meant survival, a fact that i am deeply grateful for. Today, my family and i can live indoors in a modern house with all of our needs met. (Thankfully, we live in a community with clean drinking water and safe, sturdy houses, which isn't the case for all Indigenous people in Canada.) We don't even need to walk outside and engage with nature in order to survive for a week, or perhaps two or more if we are well prepared and stocked up. However, we know that to be *well* we need fresh air. We need nature. Many of us as Indigenous people speak about wanting to make sure that our young people still know how to survive off the land (just in case). No, more than *just in case*, we want them to know because it's important to their spirit. As Indigenous people we recognize that having relationship with land, culture and traditional lifeways is more than survival—it makes us feel empowered and healthy. If our ancestors of long ago visioned forward to us now, i wonder if they would tell us that part of being a human is to be connected to the natural world and how that will never cease, no matter what kind of technology comes into the social realm.

I believe that oral storytelling is an elemental human tradition that will never completely pass away. I think it has just the same primal attraction as sitting around a campfire. I've worked with my partner, Frank, facilitating various workshops. It's quite amazing that no matter the personalities or experience of the people sitting around that circle, if they are city people or camping people, or if they are Nova Scotians or from another country anywhere in the world, everyone feels attracted to the glow and movement of that fire. As if fire speaks to us, to the very depths of our humanity in ancestral memory. I wonder how many fires kept people alive through the millennia and all around the world.

So, too, when we share a story and others listen in real time, in real space right in front of each other, our minds and hearts are triggered somewhere deep and anciently human. Oral storytelling must be as old as humans. Stories have been used as teaching mechanisms, for entertainment, for ceremony and much more.

As Indigenous Peoples we have heard time and time again that our cultures are orally based, and yet so much of our education system is through the literary tradition of European colonial cultures. I feel that both—literary and oral—have gifts and challenges about them. Through the teachings of Elders Albert and Murdena Marshall about Etuaptmumk (Two-Eyed Seeing) in Mi'kma'ki, we are meant to continue our work in today's world with at least two world views woven together for the benefit of all. Usually, in ecological conversations we mean to weave the mainstream science perspective and our cultural perspective. In my arts work as a storyteller, writer and playwright, i mean to weave and practise in both the literary and the oral. I have worked hard to strengthen my ability to listen, learn and repeat by auditory-oral methods. This rebalancing has been invaluable to me as an artist and human. In this era of hand-held devices and recorders, it's too easy to rely on technology to help us remember instead of strengthening our own body. I believe, like the need to go outside even if we have the privileged comforts to stay indoors, we need to use our oral tradition to stay healthy.

In the future, Indigenous storytellers and theatre artists will have reclaimed that ancient tradition in new ways for their modern era. Just think—they could do just about anything with oral storytelling! There could be beautifully crafted outdoor, but intimate, circular theatres that host oral storytelling competitions, performances, ceremonies and oratories as teachings. I can imagine that as one person moves around the circle, speaking their Indigenous language, audience members of all walks of life will be able to use technology to decipher/translate that language into their own, or a physical language like Braille. This Etuaptmumk-using technology to assist in the storytelling will make the accessibility for the people in the audience vast. The ability to merge technology and traditional oral storytelling will be used in a variety of ways, such as the narrator being able to turn our attention to holograms as inanimate or animated parts of the scene. Perhaps the narrator will move in and out of the images, becoming part of the scene and coming back out, similar to when we weave between narrator and character in today's storytelling.

With or without the enhanced technology of images, a group of storytellers will be able to weave in and out of each other's stories so that we get a deeper sense of the complexity of interaction and story. Moving all around, the audience will bear witness to the different kinds of transformations that different characters are responding to in the performances/tellings.

Inspired by the increase in experiential motion in modern movie theatres and theme parks, i envision some story circles using technologies built into the audience seats to enhance the storytelling. There will be sounds, smells or movement in and around the seating. Some of the visuals and sensations will be used to evoke a memory of the natural world. Even if the theatre is not positioned in nature, there will be the feeling of fire in the middle of an ecological setting (such as a forest opening, grassland, seashore, riverbank, old growth forest or tundra). In this way, we will be able to mix the very old historical stories and the new stories in a way that we had never thought was possible. This will help to keep our histories alive in the imaginations of our children.

I should say here that i have faith we will not destroy all of our natural areas in the future and that there will be storytelling and communities still living in nature. What i envision is that if the story theatre is not located in nature, the technology will exist to recreate those images for the audience. We will have these choices and abilities in the future. The choices will also allow for various forms of storytelling-audience spaces, so that instead of box theatres there will be many varieties of shapes and styles of presenting and experiencing. And every Indigenous community will have an outdoor-indoor storytelling space of their own design.

The tradition of story cycles will persist as well, where the families will come back to the storytelling circle each week for further episodes of tricksters and animals learning their way about the world. The storytellers will continue to interact with the listeners, to keep the audience involved in the telling, just as i read about in the old missionary account of our L'nu oratories. The tellers will pause and ask the audience, then, "E'e!"—the audience chimes in and demonstrates that they are attentive to the narrators and actors.

Through all of these options for interweaving technology and orality, personal presence and supports, it will be even more difficult in the future to be sure about the categories of performance art. I remember attending the Native Theatre School in Ontario back when i was a wee new adult, and our Indigenous teachers wove dance, song, story, ceremony, movement and other narrative arts all together. People would later say that they heard i had taken theatre training. I would reply, "It was all kinds of performance." That blending will continue into the future so that we will not know how to categorize oral storytelling versus video or theatre and so on. Perhaps again it will be through the re-emergence of the old traditions into new forms that we need not categorize our art.

In this future that is realigned with the importance of orality, i hope that in the education systems all children will be encouraged to use their auditory and oral senses. Sometimes the students will be asked to practise techniques of learning-by-deep-listening instead of writing notes or reading from a textbook. They will listen, imagine and store into their developing memories the teachings of their educators and peers. The students will be asked to create oral stories in the mind and perform/share them without the use of memory tools. For example, instead of children only being tested on their essay-writing ability in English class or how well they've memorized written texts, they will be required to also demonstrate their oral learning by being able to listen to an Elder a few times, synthesize the teaching in their mind and then turn to their peer and recount some of what they have heard or learned.

There will be moments during the week when the children will be asked to stand up and share their stories, using their memories or imagination. The education system is doing this because it understands the necessary biology of learning by listening, visualizing context and meaning, then being able to recount the stories or teachings, using the muscular neurons in this way. The children's brains are kept active and alert.

Each year, every child practises telling the story of their lineage and/or territory. As they age, they work on more details and going further back in time or more in-depth about their cultural histories. When they mix up the details or lose track, the adults assist, and the child revises the story in their mind. Each year, they grow their orality of their own history more clearly. On graduation from youth into adult life, they are invited to present who they are to the world, with only their memory to carry them. This means that at marriage ceremonies the full stories of the couple can be retold, as their individual lineages now merge.

In our fixed dependence on the literary tradition, orality could be misunderstood today as being a superficial learning. I've been taught that, like reading, listening to stories in whatever form is only the beginning of true learning about any subject. From that relationship, any learner must engage through time and various facets with the subject, with their hands, minds, heart, spirits and experience, in order to come to know about that subject more deeply. True, it is not enough to tell stories, but we know that stories can be the beginning, the teacher, the guide, the inspiration and the mechanism to remember and analyze further learning.

Our descendants will remember that although recording, writing and capturing images of our stories is useful, it also immobilizes the story's spirit and prevents it from being able to naturally adapt to the audience and time. Even in the future, therefore, there will be some stories that you can only listen to in that space around the fire, huddled together by the smoke. Our descendants will remember to carry some old legends in various forms, but over time they will have recrafted some of the stories we know today as fixed in character. Perhaps Kluscap's tales will have a different hero to walk among the giants and speak to all animals and people. And maybe by then, women, two-spirited and gender-neutral characters will have made their way back to our stories including as leaders, healers and guides. We and our trials today will be their "old" stories.

What i see in our future isn't only that orality will become much more popular, but that the stories we tell in the future will be the stories not only of our ancestors' survival and teachings, and not only of the European colonial history that brought about much challenge and trauma, but also of celebrating you and me and the work we're doing right now. I also imagine and hope that the stories our descendants will tell in the future will be about their lives, their struggle to understand humanity. Their stories will be about new challenges and conversations, already having enriched the diversity of story to a deeper extent than we thought was conceivable.

I hope that in the future our descendants will not need to tell stories of war because they will have learned how to make peaceful resolutions around how to share, how to honour and how to live respectfully with each other and the land. Our descendants will have remembered their traditional teachings from all around the globe about how to share the medicines they carry. I hope that in the future, stories of systemic racism are merely stories of a past long gone. And that they won't underestimate oral story, as they know stories once held up Treaties between nations when paper wasn't enough.

i heard the singing
through the fire
stones, trees, wind
and it helped me dream

so that today i may awake
and sing, too,
for those yet to be

i hope they will hear us
one day
calling out the stories
they will need to know
and the songs to help them
rise

Once i know that Frank's introductory storytelling is a few minutes from its usual end, i make an excuse to leave the circle. Outside the wi'kuom, i dress in a different shawl, wig and hat. I wait. When i hear Frank ask if the hermit is around, i hobble into the wi'kuom, full of plants and stories. I talk about the people who came before us and the lessons they left us, in code, through story. I walk around the fire and let my voice rise and fall, my arms moving about to capture their attention. I sing to them. And then i ask them to dream up the next seven generations.

Maybe the "me tomorrow" storyteller will be much like me now, gathering a small number of people in a modern wi'kuom around a fire on the bare ground, taking the talking stick and standing up to tell their story. Like the best kinds of medicines, sometimes the most effective and powerful things are the simple, natural and ancient ways that will outlive us all.

# Seventh-Generational Thinking—Fact or Fiction?

**CLARENCE LOUIE**
Chief of Osoyoos Indian Band

*I am tired of talk that comes to nothing. It makes my heart sick when I remember all the good words and the broken promises. There has been too much talk by men who had no right to talk. Good words will not get my people a home where they can live in peace and take care of themselves.*
—Chief Joseph

CHIEF JOSEPH SAID THOSE WORDS TO GOVERNMENT officials over 120 years ago as he and his people were being forced onto a reservation at gunpoint. For the past forty years, I have sat around hundreds of meetings with Chiefs, and it's very frustrating to still hear variations on "good words and promises" for a better tomorrow from Native leadership to their own people, the same speeches not backed up with action and measurable results. "Good words and promises" are said on every Rez of the 634 First Nations in Canada, especially around election time. Yet why are so many First Nations still messed up and living in poverty, with Great Depression unemployment rates (30% or more unemployed), election after election, decade after decade? It's the new millennium—time to check the past and produce, for all your membership to see, an honest "scorecard." Tell the truth. Real change always starts with facing up to the truth. Is your community dependent or independent? Is your Rez going in the right direction and improving (learning and earning), or staying messed up?

Now, no Rez is perfect and neither is any individual. We can all improve and learn more and do more. There is a saying in business that "what gets measured gets done." But where the heck are we going to end up seven generations from now? Seventh-generational thinking is supposed to be a core principle of traditional decision making: before making any major decisions, we think of the impacts seven generations ahead. We must properly plan our future—not just for one generation, our kids, and not even just for our grandkids, but for seven generations into the future.

Natives are good at talking about the past, and some (though not all) actually use lessons from the past as a guide for the future. But the sad fact is that most usually pay lip service to the future. Natives say they care about the future, yet often only Facebook-yack about it, or politically grandstand at some meeting and give the usual "I care" speech: I care about the youth, I care about the Elders, I care about our language and culture, I care about housing and education—I care—I care—I care. No real strategic planning. No real business planning. No financial planning. Smart people who truly care about the future actually put their money where their mouth is. Smart people actually do their homework and don't just yack; they figure out what their good words actually cost and put in place a financial plan.

I am a continuing student of Native Studies (now called Indigenous Studies in universities), even though I've been out of university for forty years. But through my thirty-six years as Chief of the Osoyoos Indian band I have been in the real-world reality of Native Studies. No one knows it all, no one "walks on water" (though some think they do). Real leadership knows that one needs to keep on reading, researching and learning. There is truth in the saying, "Leaders are readers." I am also an avid reader of leadership and personal development books, as my personal library will show. One of the best leadership and personal development books (and training courses) is Steven Covey's *The Seven Habits of Highly Effective People.* Habit 2 is "Begin with the end in mind"—now *that* is seventh-generational thinking. And Habit 7, "Sharpen the saw," is expressing and exercising all four dimensions of every human being— physical, social, spiritual and physical—regularly. Natives also talk of quadrants through the medicine wheel teach- ings—the physical, mental, emotional and spiritual—and the interconnectivity of all aspects of one's being, including the connection with the natural world.

In order to properly plan for a promising Rez future, we need not only traditional teachings but also modern teachings. As Native communities, we have to do some strategic planning, put in place budget controls, do a SWOT analysis, identifying strengths, weaknesses, opportun- ities and threats, in order to plan for the future. In the "Indian way," the typical SWOT analysis must also include a segment on language, heritage and culture—not just the usual modern community needs and wants. First Nations communities need modern comforts, but we also need to balance those with traditional needs and heritage and cultural protection.

In order to improve the quality of life on the Rez in the twenty-first century, we only need to focus on a handful of things, in keeping with the Pareto principle, which teaches that 80 percent of outcomes result from 20 percent of all causes for any given event in business. So focus on a few things and you will improve 80 percent of all the issues your community needs to deal with. There is no need to complicate things with a long list. Everyone who has experience with meetings knows that the more people at a meeting, the less gets done. Ever notice that long to-do lists seldom get done? There is no need for the 94 Calls to Action from the Truth and Reconciliation Commission (2015), or the 440 recommendations from the Royal Commission on Aboriginal Peoples (1996). Those are only two of many very costly studies on Native issues and "closing the socio-economic" gap. The fact is that everything on every list will cost lots of money, and all of these studies call for the usual "government needs to give Natives a lot more funding" approach.

There is a popular saying to the effect that it is better to teach someone how to fish than to give them a fish. Now isn't that the truth? I will list four common-sense real-world-reality things our people should be working toward in order to have a better tomorrow. Do these things and 80 percent of the issues on your Rez will get better, just by getting shit done right! To the critics: It's not the 100 percent solution, but the fact is that there is no 100 percent solution. A wise old war veteran said to me in a ceremony, "Don't wait for things to be perfect. Our people need things now and change now. Perfect does not exist. And don't wait for everyone to agree, or nothing will get done (except the usual one step forward, two steps back), and change for the good will not happen!"

FIRST, REMEMBER THAT everything you say you care about costs money. How much money are you setting aside for your future and your retirement? Do you have a pension, or savings? How much money are you setting aside for your kids' and grandkids' education (college or university) fund? The fact is, you and your Rez are going to need a lot more money in the future than you do now. Costs go up, not down. Good words alone will not prepare you or your community for the future. Remember: good words do not pay the bills. First Nations need to have a financial plan that supports their communities' future needs and desires. Maybe seventh-generational thinking is too far off in the future to make it relevant for most skins. Maybe thinking or making decisions based on seven generations ahead is just more Indian "rah–rah" BS, nice words with no backbone. The sad fact is that some "Rezskins" don't even pay their monthly rent. That really shows how much future thinking the ones who rip their band off do; they can't even plan ahead to deal with one month's bills (eye roll). I really wish First Nations communities would think seven generations ahead, but I rarely see it in action; I hear only phony words.

Those of us on the Rez who have kids and grandkids should at the very least be able to think, plan and save money for two generations ahead. Come on, "Indian Up" and at least sacrifice for your kids and grandkids. Keep at least one foot in the real world. How much money do you need each month to give you and your family a decent quality of life right now? That is a very easy fact (not an opinion) to figure out. Remember, there is a huge difference between having an opinion (especially an uneducated opinion) and making decisions based on fact. As Bill Bullard, a former member of the Michigan legislature, wrote, "Opinion is really the lowest form of human knowledge. It requires no accountability, no understanding."

You cannot plan for the future without getting the financial facts on how much money your First Nation is spending this month to maintain all the programs and services it provides. Community spending is another very easy fact to get. Now multiply that by twelve and add inflation and it's not hard to figure out future financial costs. Natives have a very bad habit of talking and coming up with lofty, tear-jerking ideas without figuring out what reality costs. Remember, dreaming and visioning is free, but reality always costs money. It is stupid to even talk about the future without first putting down on paper a few important facts about today. First Nations need financial independence, and they've gotta make their own self-earned income and not depend on or wait for government grants.

For my Rez, the Osoyoos Indian Band Development Corporation mission statement is "Working with business to preserve our past by strengthening our future." That means that in order to be an independent community in the future, we need to be financially and economically strong now, with our own sources of revenue and enough jobs to support our people. Being on welfare is not a good future for anyone—especially kids. Jobs and revenue are where opportunities for our people come from. Not phony Rez speeches and empty promises. And in order to preserve our past, we also need money to pay for those language, heritage and culture programs. The fact is, everything costs money. Words alone do not pay for language and cultural programs. Every cultural program I know of costs thousands of dollars. Every environmental program I know of costs money. I don't know one environmentalist who works for free. Hunting rifles, boats and fishing gear are not free. No one and no organization can put food on their plate or properly feed their future generations without money in their bank account. An individual and a community both need to make more money and have a savings account for the future. Do not talk about the future unless you're also going to talk about how much money you're going to need to live comfortably in the future. The fact is, the future is not free.

I give a Rez shout-out to those few First Nations that have put seventh-generational thinking into action by setting up trust funds to protect the short- and long-term needs of their community. Part of the "I care" speech is always about education. The fact is, education is very expensive. At Osoyoos we buck up over $200,000 out of self-generated income to go toward today's educational needs. Annual educational needs twenty to forty years from now are going to be well over half a million dollars. A few forward-thinking First Nations have set up education trust funds. One of the best examples of setting aside money for future generations is the Navajo Nation Trust Fund. It started in 1985 with $217 million from a court settlement. The leadership did not cave in to pressure to split it up on a per-capita basis, and today the Navajo Nation Trust Fund is worth over $3 billion and earns over $70 million a year for today's and tomorrow's community needs. Wow! Now that's doing it right!

When looking a few generations ahead, therefore, increasing your band's bank account must be a priority. I know most Rezskins don't have much of a savings account, and the ones who care and plan for their financial future do. I know spending money is easy but making money and saving money requires intelligence and discipline. Remember, no matter who stands up in a public meeting or writes on Facebook how much they care about Rez issues, you can only do what you can afford to do, and not having enough cash will always stop cheap, political me-me talk.

SECOND, INCREASE YOUR community land base. I believe land is more important than money. But you cannot buy more land if you do not have the money. Don't depend on loonie auctions and selling 50/50 tickets to raise money to buy land. You gotta have land leases, business income, or land settlement or natural resource development agreements (mining, oil, gas, forestry, fishing, etc.). At Osoyoos, we are over four thousand acres short of our original reserve size. So, like many First Nations in Canada and the United States, we are using self-generated income to buy back land. To date, Osoyoos has bought over eight hundred acres. Some land purchases are for increased economic development (protecting our future), but some are also for cultural purposes (hunting and fishing). A strong First Nation must have a land base from which to build a strong sustainable community. All First Nations must start making more money and buying land to increase their Rez land base. Obviously, our membership is growing: we are Canada's youngest and fastest-growing population. In order to look after a growing population, therefore, adding to your Rez land base must be a priority.

It's awesome to see hundreds of "additions to reserves" being created all across the country—some through land claims, some through Treaty Land Entitlement claims, and some through the common-sense fact that our Indian reserves need to get bigger to accommodate future growth and opportunities. At Osoyoos we have been buying land both on and off the Rez. Every Rez should have a "land purchase" budget. If your Rez is still the same size ten to twenty years from now, then your leadership messed up an important part of their responsibilities for the future. As Native people, we always talk about how important the land is, how the land defines who we are as a people. So buck up and buy some of it back. Don't sit around and wait for white people or government to give it back, 'cause that just ain't gonna happen.

The future is going to demand more money and land—that's a given.

THIRD, EVERY COMMUNITY must improve on its "communities culture." After those first two priorities (remember, as one Chief so rightly said, "Everything on the Rez is a priority"), there must be people development. The atmosphere created over time in your home, office or community is its culture. You can do all the modern strategic planning you want, but do not forget that "culture eats strategy for breakfast." Every Rez needs to improve its "Rez culture." If your community has greedy, lying, corrupt leadership, it's because your community has the same negative culture based on greed, hate and corruption. We need to get back to the hard-working, tell-the-truth-at-all-times culture of our ancestors. Every First Nation comes from a "working culture." Before the English and French came into our territories and forced our people onto Indian reserves, we were self-supporting people. Natives worked hard for a living, every day of every year. Think about it: it was hard work to provide food, clothing and shelter for a family when there were no grocery stores, no electricity, no clothing stores. No one else built your family's house to live in—you built and maintained your home yourself. Every family had to build and maintain its own home, make its own clothes, and hunt and gather food every day. Our people did not depend on handouts or hang around forts for rations. Our ancestors got up early (did not sleep till noon) and worked hard every day to provide food, clothing and shelter.

Getting back to a "working culture" is key for a community development. No lazy asses, no entitlement attitude. I heard a wise, hard-working Native leader say, "We need to move from a culture of entitlement to a culture of performance." That means we get back to standing on our own two feet, going to school, getting a job, and "earning and learning." It also means being responsible for your own situation and your own house and yard. A majority of people in a Rez community must reset the culture of their community. A community's culture does not just mean a traditional culture. Every office has a culture, every school has a culture, sports has its own culture. Culture is a way of doing things, with protocols and unwritten codes of conduct. So every Rez has a culture. I want my Rez culture to be one of "learning and earning," where in every household kids wake up seeing at least one adult going to work every working day. Role-modelling is so important. Kids should not be raised in a house where adults don't work or don't get up early and get busy doing something productive.

Drug and alcohol abuse also has its own culture. And the sad fact is that the drug and alcohol culture has existed on most First Nations for generations. Drugs and alcohol are still with us, and we must come up with new ways to loosen their grip on some of our people. The drugs today are more dangerous and addicting, and the hard drugs are more dangerous than alcohol. First Nations need to share their successes and failures in the ongoing war on drugs. The culture of drug dealing is among the biggest problems on most Rezzes.

Culture is also about how community members talk to each other and resolve differences. There will always be differences in politics on the Rez and differences in opinion on all issues. Native communities do not think and act the same on any issue. The basis of Rez politics is "who gets what—when and how." There must be fair, transparent and honest communication at all times. We must improve on how we engage with each other so we don't have a culture of "civil war," always fighting and arguing with each other over differences. Mature adults can have business manners and "agree to disagree." Too many First Nations Rez cultures today are based on lies, threats and mafia-style intimidation. I still hear about how some Chiefs and Councils are not fair and honest, and band office staff play favourites and ignore policies and procedures. There is no decent future for a community that still has an "Indian crab syndrome," where members don't like seeing anyone with new vehicles or succeeding and, like crabs in a bucket, when one tries to climb out, the others pull them back in. Many Native communities operate with a culture of bullying and take, take and take. The Rez culture needs to be one of honour, caring, sharing and respect. The bottom line is that culture does matter.

FOURTH, REAL "LEADERSHIP" is needed in every Rez community. John C. Maxwell, one of the world's experts on leadership, wrote, "Everything rises and falls on leadership."[1] That is a real-world fact. Your community is where it's at because of past and present elected leadership. The sad fact is that there is a lack of real leadership in Indian country. Too many phony politicians and not enough genuine leaders. As much as Natives complain about colonization and what white people have done to us, Rez elections sure are beginning to look more and more like white elections, with all the campaign letters, signs and debates, and the Facebook trashing and mudslinging. Traditionally, Native leadership was based on performance, not speeches or Facebook rants. I know that many Tribes' words for their leaders translated into "those who are of the nice." That's so awesome. All Native leaders should have embedded in their hearts, as their core principle, that they truly are "of the nice." Because if you are "of the nice," you will not call others down, you will not lie, you will live a hard-working, giving life. The fact is that people are generally either takers or givers. In order for a community to move forward in a good way, the majority of its staff and leaders must be givers, not takers.

We need to quit mirroring white people's elections and look back at how our Tribes developed leaders, and

.................

1      John C. Maxwell, *The 21 Indispensable Qualities of a Leader: Becoming the Person Others Will Want to Follow* (Nashville: Thomas Nelson, 2007).

not model the contemporary name-calling, lies and fake-news election politics of today. I tell youth, don't base your vote on phony speeches and what candidates say or write—promises and personal grandstanding on Facebook are easy to make, and phony politicians love to make promises. Base your vote on what they have done in your community. What job do they now hold (and do they even work)? How long have they proved themselves as a good worker? Do they attend community functions regularly (or only around election time)? Do they volunteer their own time? Do they put their own money toward fundraising efforts all year round, or only around election time? Be aware of the phony "I care about the community" types who only pop their heads out of the sand around election time. Elect hard-working people, not people who promise to work hard. Elect nice people, with a good work record, not people who promise to be fair and open-minded. Don't elect people who don't pay their own bills.

And if your Rez is in a messed-up state, then look at the present leadership. Remember, "Everything rises and falls on leadership." For your community to have a decent tomorrow, your community must elect people with positive energy, not negative energy. A person's employment and school record is an important part of their "personal score card." Leaders by definition are out front and "doers" who get things done. Remember, that is what leaders do: they get things done.

It is very important to remember that leaders are not only those who are elected. Leaders are managers and department heads and all those in important business and social services positions in a community who, every day of every week, collect a paycheque for improving their community. From daycare staff to all those employed in social services and business—these are leadership positions. The main question is, are they earning their paycheque and making their community better, or are they just collecting a paycheque and not improving things? Are they civil servants, working for the betterment of the community, or are they just working for themselves and their own family and friends? If things on the Rez are not improving, then some people are holding important leadership positions and not performing. In the real world, slackers get their butts fired—"cuzzins" included!

On a Rez, everything is intertwined, and a weakness or a slacker in one position affects others. In the future, we need to improve all aspects of the Rez organizational structure and have a scorecard for every position that affects the future well-being of our communities. Leadership and governance are the foundation of Nation building. A messed-up community means its leadership and governance are messed up.

Seventh-generational thinking means Nation building or Nation rebuilding. I don't mean becoming mirror images of corporate Canada or the corporate United States. An unorganized, dysfunctional brown bureaucracy is no better than a white bureaucracy. At the Rez level we need to incorporate some First Nations traditional values and conduct into our Rez governments.

Search out best practices in Indian country. Don't act like you're an island unto yourself or you're in your own unique "bubble." Many of the things we have incorporated in our business and social programs at Osoyoos we learned from other First Nations on both sides of the Canada–U.S. border. There are many ways to improve your community and plan for what your Rez needs to do to get it right, and some of the answers already exist in other communities. So be a student of other First Nations—the good, the bad, and the ugly.

"ME TOMORROW" IS a very important idea because the future does start with you. Change always starts individually and then branches out to others in a family and then a community. I want to think about the future of my Rez first individually—what I can do to make things better—and then the handful of things leadership needs to focus on, as everything is eventually intertwined. What you do in one area will affect other areas to the good or the bad. As a Rez, we really do need more "we" thinking than "me" thinking.

As The Greatest, boxing champ Muhammad Ali, once said, quoting the African proverb, "If there is no enemy within, the enemy outside can do you no harm."

And from one of the greatest Chiefs of all time, who lived through the toughest of times and gave us a real "we tomorrow" direction, Sitting Bull: "Let us put our minds together and see what life we can make for our children."

# Our Education
# Tomorrow

**SHELLEY KNOTT FIFE**
Education Specialist & PhD Candidate[1]

E DUCATION NEEDS IN INDIGENOUS COMMUNITIES ARE AS varied as the characteristics of the different Indigenous groups across Turtle Island itself. Each community, like each individual student, will have a need that is specific to them. My personal journey has had me exploring what tomorrow's education could look like and why it is important that it look like *our* education. I was raised from birth on my home reserve in Ontario. My professional career in Indigenous education has spanned over twenty years, from managing a First Nation education department to working as a consultant with a provincial school board to interpreting and codeveloping First Nations education policy change at provincial and federal levels. My children and I were educated on reserve. Since the 1960s I've witnessed the evolution of control over schools on reserve. As a student and as an adult, I've seen a federally controlled school

..................

1       I am currently a PhD candidate, and much of this chapter is from various submissions meeting course writing requirements.

on reserve morph into a provincially controlled school—
that is, a "school of the provincial board"—and finally to
a band-operated school. These developments occurred
because of the will of the people in the community. All
levels of management on reserve are federally funded, but
program and policy management are now controlled by the
First Nation with a band-operated school. Federal program
guidelines still exist but have become increasingly broad
and more flexible in scope.

To expand on my personal journey, my very young
childhood was sheltered, and we were not really allowed
to play much beyond the sight of my parents. It was a time
when a parental look and stern warning was all that was
required as a virtual "fence." It was a time of very lush
green grass, leafy trees and calm, clean water. We were
sheltered and closely watched, and I don't think anyone
was conscious of why. My dad's four older siblings, ranging
in age from about six to ten years old at the time they were
taken, were driven to the Shingwauk Residential School in
Sault Ste. Marie by the "black car" that could legally come
and grab children. It was not so long before the time I was
born that that black car still roamed the village. I remember being cleaned very roughly, especially on the elbows,
and having hairbrushes taken to the hair, in order to avoid
being called "dirty" by the zhaagnosh who were tourists
in the village, or if we were to be so lucky as to catch the
weekly bus or a car ride into town.

My paternal grandparents were gone before we came
along, but I had the privilege, and grace, to be gifted with
amazing maternal grandparents, Donald and Clay, who
had the ability to make their thirty-plus grandchildren and
step-grandchildren each feel like they were the only one.

They left a legacy of family and humour with their fourteen children. At their house, the kitchen table chatter was rich in Anishinaabemwin, as nearly every one of the fourteen siblings were fluent in the language, though none of us children were encouraged to speak in Anishinaabe—to further "shelter" us from the punishment that they experienced in school for simply speaking the language or from the still lingering threat of that black car.

Our community, not just family, was close. My grandparents were among the first to get a colour TV in the village, and people from far and wide gathered in the living room of their old white house to watch it. They were the first down our way to get a bathroom and, like little ducks behind our mom, we would walk down there on Saturdays for a bath, no longer having to heat the tub on the woodstove. Good times. They really were.

Coming from two of the biggest families in the village, my dad's siblings numbered eleven. I easily have over sixty first cousins, that I know of, and, with in-laws, probably a hundred. Community and family to me were one and same; if you were not a first cousin, chances were you were second, third, tenth.

Our roads around the village were just dirt roads. Until I was about eight or nine years old, our little three-room house had not yet been bricked. We had no indoor plumbing, and there was a huge wood stove for heating and cooking. This was normal for pretty much all the homes in the village. Having a November birthday, I began school at the age of five, and I cannot recall using an indoor toilet before I attended Grade 1 at the Mud Lake Indian Day School on reserve. Like most people, I do not have an awareness of memories before the age of four, so my brightest first memories are of flush toilets. And the school had a flush toilet. If you have ever had to use an outhouse—in the winter especially—you will appreciate this fixation. I remember conversations with my dad when I was that young, in Grades 1 and 2, about how things in "town" and in zhaagnosh houses seemed different, and he would refer to the mysterious "Indian Act." Indigenous political awakenings were gaining momentum at that time, as Indigenous people, primarily Status Indians, became part of the modern political presence as a result of being made voting members of Canada in the year I was born, 1960. Possessing voting rights garnered political attention, and in less than a decade, before I was a teenager, I saw our gravel roads become paved, our dark nights being lit by streetlights and our tar-papered three-room house gain brick walls, four bedrooms, a bathtub with running water and . . . a flush toilet.

During that time of modernization in our village, a cultural regeneration was starting. Coming out of the era of outlawed traditional ceremony and practice, our powwows had resembled fair-like events, with a stage to allow us to display ourselves in our regalia. In hindsight, our exercises in finding those traditional practices were a struggle. In the centennial year, 1967, our village received money to purchase deer hide to run a project where families, generally the women, could make buckskin dresses. Because of restricted movement off and on reserve, actual hunting was not happening as much as today or as abundantly. My mom made one for herself and one for me. I was six going on seven at the time, so my dress lasted until I was in my early teens, and then I started to wear the one my mom made for herself. It now hangs in my living room. I remember that once I had regalia, there were conversations with the Elders, and a book even surfaced with old traditional dance steps. I am grateful for Elders like Great-Aunt Gladys Taylor and Uncle Johnny Jacobs, who patiently worked with us kids to rejuvenate our peoples' love of the drum and dance. It was a time when Anishinaabe could begin the journey back to our ways of the drum and when gatherings no longer had to resemble a fair to avoid persecution. It was like learning to walk again; I remember looking at that book to see how our people used to dance. Some people look back and kind of mock how the powwow used to be, with a stage and all, but like I said, our people were waking up from that time when our heritage at large was made to sleep. My Great-Aunt Gladys and my Uncle Johnny took great pains to teach us how to paddle dance, for example, at that time. "Are we going fast or slow this time, Lou," I would ask my childhood best friend.

My academic career began early as I loved school and faced real social pains because of that passion, having been taken behind the local "Indian Day School" by my friends a couple of times as they pounded into me that they didn't appreciate my eagerness to learn this foreign stuff. School was my escape from my sheltered life. I loved to learn of the world, and I was intrigued by the Beaver Cleaver life I was seeing in black and white on the little screen. Busing into nearby Lakefield for Grade 4 was like going to the moon, and I wanted to know all about this outside place. While we did tend to huddle in our little Anishinaabe mass at the new school, I remember my mother's words to me: "Now make friends with everybody." A pivotal moment for me was when we were to pick partners for a project and my Anishinaabe friends were looking at me like, "You're picking me, right?" and I chose a white friend that I had just made. I

guess I did heed my mom's advice because I ended up win-
ning the "citizenship" award that first year. It was years
before I understood what that year meant. Oxfam defines
global citizenship as being aware of and understanding the
wider world—and one's place in it. Global citizens take an
active role in their community. Our village and my family
have always understood that the Canadian landscape was
changing and that we needed education and an understanding of the ways of this changing world to determine
how best to navigate it. My parents always stressed that
whatever we did, we needed to return to community and
give back. I figured that my place was to have one foot
in each world, to see how harmony could exist and how I
could contribute to the greater community. A young me did
not know about the missionary or other colonial influen-
ces on our reserve, which translated into the reality that
I'd be accepted as long as I was speaking English and not
Anishinaabe, learning settler protocols and only wearing
my "Indianness" in a non-threatening, reticent way. Over
the years, I became more and more aware that I was not
helpless and was very capable of ascending to wherever I
needed and wanted to be in this colonized society, appre-
ciating my role as an educator. This realization is why I
completely identify with what Lila Watson, an Australian
Aborigine, has said: "If you have come to help me, you are
wasting your time. But if you have come because your liberation is bound up with mine, then let us work together."

There is good news in that an optimal place of
learning is being created in some degree in many First
Nations today. While many communities likely do not have
the desired physical structure that encompasses all that
they dream of within their desired "learning lodge," our

communities have worked with what we've had at hand since time immemorial and have strived to manifest the journey of meaningful lifelong learning. There is often the misconception that a place of learning is completely based on a desire to return to the past, when actually it is a desire to bring the meaning of who Indigenous people are at a foundational level up here to the present, to be well established for tomorrow. For too long, the original cultures of this land have been suppressed and not celebrated as a contributing presence to the modern-day culture of Canada. It has not been understood that this is the homeland of Canada's original people, and I stress the *homeland*. This is the only place in this world where Anishinaabe, Haudensaunee, Dene or Inuktitut languages, for example, still live or can ever hope to be retrieved. This is the land where the Seven Grandfather Teachings and the Great Law of Peace originated. First Nations, Métis and Inuit people exist because of this land, in this place.[2]

Indigenous people know this belonging, to the land, to this place, in the very heart of their being. The struggle has been to rise above the systemic efforts at work to eliminate this knowing. This struggle has involved retrieving the tools of our knowing. These tools originated where we thrived—in community, in extended family, on the land. A learning place of tomorrow would be an extension of that sense of place, surrounded by the family of community.

Our return to family, to the haven of a safe community—wherever that community may be, as there are many

....................

2     Fife, S. K. (2008, September). "Nurturing the First Nation, Metis and Inuit Spirit in Our Schools." Peterborough, Ontario: Kawartha Pine Ridge District School Board.

urban Indigenous communities that are well established and have no intention of moving—would justly serve the future well-being of our people. It is still too easy for Indigenous people to be targeted in the justice and penal systems. It is still too easy for our children to be apprehended and taken into care. Could a return to ourselves on a large scale thwart the overrepresentation of Indigenous people in these systems? Ryan Beardy, a reformed survivor of the prison system, thinks so, as he found family and community in less than desirable places before turning his life around.[3] Family support is a critical piece for successful education systems, as parents and caregivers need help in supporting their young learners.

When non-Indigenous people hear of the desire of our communities to become decolonized, they often think that it means a desire to return to living in precontact conditions, without today's technologies or conveniences. While the return of pristine, natural environments is likely desirable, the overall assumption that we would want to physically live unlike others in society is usually not true. Ultimately, the desire is to have our world views, life principles and established constitutions acknowledged and coexisting with or even incorporated into today's societal norms. It could be said that Indigenous communities simply want their value systems to have agency and not just to have identities and societies based in myths or folklore. The contribution of Indigeneity to today's world and the establishment of enduring Indigenous education systems

..................

3        R. Beardy, "Family Matters: Home Is at the Heart of the Indigenous Prison Crisis," *The Globe and Mail*, October 20, 2020.

depends on us advancing away from preservation mode, studying and then "storing away" our culture or viewing it as not being viable in everyday life. Our original knowledge—for example, our understanding of the natural world and how to best live in it[4,5]—needs to be revitalized, nurtured and instilled in our young generations and those to come.

This returning to ourselves, or Biskaabiyang,[6,7] reminds us to put our Indigeneity at the centre of all we do. To remember who we are in our teachings. Remembering brings back our belief in our connectedness with each other, with all things. Wonderfully, there is a growing academy of educators who can show us how to put the remembering first. In "Braiding Histories," Susan Dion gives a practical demonstration of the transformation of teaching practices using Indigenous material, specifically stories, in the classroom.[8] Wendy Geniusz offers a sample of decolonized Anishinaabe Knowledge, Gikendaasowin (in

..................

4     C. Andersen, *"Métis": Race, Recognition, and the Struggle for Indigenous Peoplehood* (Vancouver, BC: UBC Press, 2014).

5     Wendy M. Geniusz, *Our Knowledge Is Not Primitive: Decolonizing Botanical Anishnaabe Teachings* (Syracuse, NY: Syracuse University Press, 2009).

6     Geniusz, *Our Knowledge Is Not Primitive.*

7     L.B. Simpson, *Dancing on Our Turtle's Back: Stories of Nishnaabeg Re-Creation, Resurgence and a New Emergence* (Winnipeg, MB: Arbeiter Ring, 2011).

8     Susan Dion, *Braiding Histories: Learning from Aboriginal Peoples' Experiences and Perspectives: Including the Braiding Histories Stories* (Vancouver, BC: UBC Press, 2009).

the chapter "Giizhikaatig miinawaa Wiigwaasi-mitig") a whole story/writing/teaching of the medicines and gifts of the Northern White Cedar and of the Birch Tree, including songs, stories of origin and recipes for the medicines.[9]

Traditionally, knowledge, skills, values and morals were transferred primarily through oral instruction and modelling. Storytelling was a means to relay expectations in behaviour and societal roles.[10] Children were given as much time as they needed to achieve success when attempting a new skill. Progress and achievement were not measured in percentages or numerical values. An Elder I know once proclaimed that he would hate to see the student who only learned fifty percent of how to paddle his canoe across the lake.

An article in Maclean's magazine's 2021 university rankings issue highlights the merits of gradeless—that is, pass/fail—systems in post-secondary education, through encouraging and developing ethical and intellectual values for learning. This creates less stress and more well-being in students. In gradeless systems, more emphasis is placed on qualitative values. The article speaks to students searching—in the pursuit of good grades—for easily passible courses to increase their grade point average rather than taking a course that might actually enhance their learning in their major course of study.[11]

...................

9      Geniusz, *Our Knowledge Is Not Primitive.*

10     N.T. Bell, *Culturally Relevant Aboriginal Education* (Don Mills, ON: Pearson Canada, 2015).

11     J. Dunch, "It's time for Canadian universities to go Gradeless," *Maclean's*, October 8, 2020.

Gradeless education systems could also be a starting point for teaching students who are deemed to have learning disabilities according to quantitative-focused systems. Configuring learning scenarios according to goals that are set based on student strengths and on mastery of skills would encourage student well-being, self-esteem and self-motivating skills. Mastery of skills and scaffolded, knowledge-based intellectual development fosters the notion of education as a public good rather than solely as developing a labour market. The notion of public good was the basis of Anishinaabe communal life. A meritocracy, as it were. When I arrived at the University of Waterloo back in the dark ages, my newly introduced roommate asked me what my goals were. I simply replied that I really did not know, but I knew that whatever it was would involve going back to work for the community. If I had something to offer the community, it was expected that it would be shared. It was simply an ingrained understanding. I followed my grades and my heart and ended up in the field of Indigenous education.

A common Anishinaabe teaching is that if one of the four quadrants of the medicine wheel—representing health in Spirit, Physical Health, Intellect and Emotional Well-Being—is not quite flush or whole, the wheel does not turn properly. Our communal family requires healing in some, if not all, of the quadrants, and the education of tomorrow can help accommodate much of that healing.

First Nations community practice tends to section off various departments in silo-like formats, where education departments don't interact with health departments, for example, each perhaps focusing on expenditure of their own budgets. If all were working together, would the medicine wheel be healed? What would the education curriculum look like if the strands, fundamental concepts, and expectations were organized by medicine wheel quadrant, for example?

First Nations control of First Nations education has been in motion at the grassroots level since the 1970s, with the National Indian Brotherhood's (now the Assembly of First Nations) "Indian Control of Indian Education."[12] Transition to First Nations control involves the challenge of understanding the effects of colonization and how powerful the divide-and-conquer systems actually have been. In many cases, colonization affected community trust in a First Nation's ability to deliver educational programming that would accommodate today's societal needs. Strong co-operative leadership in all facets of community can inspire unity in achieving goals. Strategic planning is an exercise that many communities are familiar with, but implementation requires strong commitment.

"Civilized" society tends to want to "fix" biological, intellectual or environmental shortcomings to solve challenges with students at school. This need to "fix" came into play when Indigenous students were sent to Indian residential schools and taught a shockingly new curriculum that would "fix" their inability to act "white." This specific deficit thinking adversely affected not only Indigenous children and Indigenous communities but the trajectory of our people for generations.

..................

12    Chiefs of Ontario, *The New Agenda: A Manifesto for First Nation Education in Ontario* (Toronto: Chiefs of Ontario, 2005). http://education.chiefs-of-ontario.org/article/manifesto-269.asp.

In terms of trajectory, Indigenous communities have been working to regain their cultural, spiritual and communal footing. It has been said that if it takes an hour to walk into the bush, it will take an hour to walk out of the bush. The residential school system, colonial economic practices and bans on cultural practices, among many other colonialisms, affected four or five generations of Indigenous people, and we are just barely out of the first generation of non–residential school attendees, for example. It could take another three or four generations for Indigenous communities to regain that healthy medicine wheel. Much must be overcome, including, for some, the horrific experience of the colonial practices that embedded learning failures and even learning trauma into the blood memory of students, their families and their communities.

To get to the physical and celebrated place of learning what communities envision will require commitment at all levels of the community. What does the desired education system look like, and how much will it cost? Is it possible to develop a case to use existing resources plus ask for more for the desired system and, really, why wouldn't that be possible? Sadly, our communities are frequently placed in a reactive cycle, but it is time to pause and really build that which is desired. The Chiefs of Ontario developed a manifesto that outlined why there is urgency for First Nations' control and jurisdiction over education.[13] Survival of Indigenous consciousness and cultural identity is dependent on this autonomy, but our goals have to be clear.

.................

13      Chiefs of Ontario, *The New Agenda: A Manifesto for First Nation Education in Ontario* (Toronto: Chiefs of Ontario, 2005). http://education.chiefs-of-ontario.org/article/manifesto-269.asp.

In recent years, there has been advancement toward more land-based learning, with a focus on the original languages and culture-based activities. All types of curriculum, provincial or locally developed, can incorporate aspects of Indigeneity. In terms of funding requirements, there is actually no restriction on what a school year should look like, at least in Ontario. Nicole Bell, in her book *Just Do It*, beautifully outlines a seasons-based curriculum.[14]

If one were given a certain amount of money to feed oneself for a year and told to use only this one particular store that sold unsuitable food, what would the options be? Make the case, take a stand and announce that another source must be used? What would be required to make that argument? One could say that another source provided healthy food that could be used now, plus seeds that could be sown to ensure food for tomorrow. This same argument could be used for developing curricula and localized, community-based education systems that are appropriate for our communities.

Some work has been done in provincial systems to develop accurate and authentic, Indigenous-based curriculum material but not enough to even scratch the surface. Much has also been done at the local level in First Nations regarding the development of reading and other program materials written in Indigenous languages to be used in First Nations elementary schools. Diverse settings and capacity in Indigenous communities requires that education systems no longer be modelled after a monolithic,

......................

14    Nicole Bell, *Just Do It: Providing Anishinaabe Culture-Based Education* (Saarbrucken, Germany: VDM Verlag Dr. Muller Aktiengesellschaft & Co., 2010).

obstinately indivisible, one-size-fits-all invention. There are many examples across Turtle Island of genuinely intellectually challenging, high-quality programs for students in Indigenous communities. One thing that COVID-19 has provided is the opportunity to shake things up and inspire educators to dig deep into the well of creativity to work out how to accommodate all learners. In this process, educators have been provided with insights into what students need for basic learning and how that learning can be maximized in less than optimal environments like virtual classrooms. For remote communities, it is even possible that virtual learning has opened up opportunities that might not have been used in the past. Future learning may involve a continuation of prerecorded lessons, more individualized programming, and other means of creative program delivery.

Our education tomorrow will require clear communal vision and co-operation regarding goals, program composition and family support networks, and an understanding that it can be within the capacity of the community to develop that system themselves.


## KINOOMAAGEWGAMIG

Nokomis notices nojishe peeking around the corner and motions for her to come for a quick squeeze before the little girl rushes off to Kinoomaage-kwe for this morning's lessons. Nokomis is on hand most mornings at Kinoomaagewgamig to give hugs, to smile kindness, to embody and model the grandfather teachings while sharing lessons of the great relationship, that relationship between all of the beings of creation provided by the Earth Mother. Nokomis reflects on the peace that has finally descended on the community since this calming space of learning came to be. No longer would children have to travel by bus from one end of the village or even out of the village, from one square prefab building to the next. The circular structure now houses all the children in whatever stage of growing in mind and body that may be.

As she allows herself a few minutes to wander the varied spaces of Kinoomaagewgamig, the learning lodge, Nokomis marvels at the contrast of this warm space where laughter rings in the passageway between the various gathering areas designed for specific student-oriented types of teaching. As she peeks in the doorway of one room, she nods to one Kinoomaage-kwe who is revealing the skill of writing the English alphabet to a handful of children, new in discovering the world captured in printed word. While the alphabet may be English in origin, the words are Anishinaabe. Nokomis's breath catches at the sudden warmth in her heart; that should be a familiar feeling to her by now, but she is still taken aback by how often this happens. Lessons are shared while children sit in a circle. As new letters and words are introduced, one child practises the word to the child beside them, who does the same for the next child, and so on. There are giggles when one laughs at themselves in their attempt, but all in the room enjoy that personal joke. Walking to another section of the lodge, Nokomis can smell the fresh-cut pine lumber in the woodworking class and hear the soft sound of keyboards across the hall as students are learning to code. Further down the hall is a foyer of wood construction looking out onto the cooking grounds. Modern outdoor cooking facilities are juxtaposed with various firepits. Moving further out in the yard is a wide seating arrangement circling the sacred fire pit.

There is a class there now with Shomis, Grandfather, instructing the group in how to assemble the layers of a sacred fire that represent family and community and sharing why there are differences between types of fireplaces and fires. Across the small clearing beyond the fire area, a group of students is preparing to walk the kilometer or so to the marsh for today's teachings on the land. The horrible stories that Nokomis had been told by her mother of the clinical and cold school that Kob'de had attended far away from her family were becoming distant memories, shoved so far back when she wandered these bright new pathways of learning. There is healing here and joy in knowing that these Anishinaabe binoojinyag will never know a cruelty of the past.

# Don't Give Up!

**RAYMOND YAKELEYA**
Filmmaker & Writer

FOR A LONG TIME I HAVE BEEN WORRIED ABOUT THE future of not only my People, the Dene, but all Native People across Canada and in the United States. I have seen nothing but "cultural erosion" on a massive scale, as if we have forgotten our culture and traditions and not passed them on to the next generation.

Recently, I was asked where I thought our Native People would be a hundred years from now. It is a damn good question, and it left me wondering about the future. Maybe it is about time to put my wizard's hat on, look into the future and see what will become of us. It is time to use the power of our voice and written word to shake the People up on how precarious our Native cultures are in 2021, to reflect on what we have lost and what we could lose in the future. Not only that but to talk to one another, to plan the things we need to do to save and to preserve what the Creator gave us.

We must start at the beginning, when we were created by Newetsine (the Dene name for "God the Creator," which means the "One who made the World"). When I was a young boy, my dad's mom, my grandmother Elizabeth Yakeleya, explained to me that when the Creator was making our People and all others in the world, the Creator gave us all beautiful gifts to help us survive and thrive in the world we are now living in. The gifts of language, songs, communication with all animals and birds, medicinal knowledge from plants, healing, prophecy, weather knowledge, and so on. These are things we needed to help us survive an often brutal existence as our People made their way and cut their trail to North America from Siberia during the last ice age. The weather extremes and the giant animals, such as the mastodons, mammoths, dire wolves, North American lions, sabre-toothed tigers, giant beavers, cave bears and so on made this a perilous journey, where people were used as food by these predators. With our Stone Age tools and weapons, we managed to take the "dog" from the wolf and "fire" from the sky, two valuable allies, and we made our way to our places in North America to find our lands and ourselves. What an epic journey they took to discover a new continent and a new world! These were our ancestors, our grannies and grandpas, our People. This is where our story begins ...

THE DENE PEOPLE form the largest First Nations group in North America in terms of total population size and land ownership. From Alaska to Hudson Bay, south along the Pacific coast to the American Southwest and on to northern Mexico, where our relatives, the Apache and Navajo, reside—from a cold land teeming with wildlife and lots of water to a scorched land with very little water—they survived and thrived, a testament to their resilience and fighting spirit. They made their name in the annals of war, fighting to stay independent and free in a country south of our border that professed freedom and equality for all— but only if you were a white man, not a person of colour. Such falsehoods betrayed the promise of liberty for all. We still see this false narrative being played out in the burning streets of the United States today.

However, I am getting ahead of myself. Things for all North and South American First Nations took a bad turn when the Spanish conquistadores and their black-robed priests arrived in the southern hemisphere to begin their dark chapter in their New World with dreams and night-mares of stealing gold, and the killing and enslavement of innocent people in the name of civilization. They made the template for how uncivilized native people would be treated by civilized savages. Somehow, Christianity popped its head into this mix with their number one sales-man, Jesus, leading the way, doing the devil's work with the collection plate in his hand, always asking for more alms on behalf of the church. We began to see the true God of the Christians as money; the rest about saving souls is just talk. I always felt that the Northern and Southern Native cultures and values stood in the way of the Europeans right from the beginning, as the fight for the land began. The land was surely too good for us and had to be under Euro-pean control, so this began the destruction of our People.

I needed to say this in order to share my thoughts properly as I think of the future. I can also share my obser-vations from my own life and work, and my experiences with other First Nations in my life's journey.

Many years ago, when my family moved back to Fort Norman in the central Northwest Territories, from

Yellowknife, it was like stepping back into an earlier time, when there was no electricity in the homes and everything was done with a wood stove and a gas lamp—the Stone Age to my eight-year-old mind. In the winter, we would travel by dog team to get wood, and ice for water, to visit our snarelines and traplines and to hunt for moose and caribou. We wore handmade mukluks, moccasins, parkas and moosehide jackets, and we ate wild game food—rabbits, ptarmigan, ducks, geese, moose, caribou, mountain sheep, and so on. This was supplemented with store-bought supplies for making bannock and other things we needed. Life at its simplest. The People spoke the Dene language fluently, but you could already see the cultural break.

I attended a one-room school in Fort Norman until I was nine years old. When I was ten, I was sent to Grollier Hall, the dreaded Catholic-run school residence further north in Inuvik, nearer to the Arctic Ocean. It was where the Missionary Oblates of Mary Immaculate and the Grey Nuns ran their religious hostel like a military prison. It was a place where we lost our spiritual and cultural innocence and gained insight to the true intentions of the Roman Catholic Church. The horrible treatment the boys received did nothing to instill confidence in us and our cultures. "Your language is the language of the Devil and your ways are the ways of the Snake!" These famous words were spoken by the evil French-Canadian nun Sister Hébert, our chief jailer and the witch whose meanness was famous across the Beaufort region. The Oblates priest in charge did nothing to help us—except to hire four pedophile male supervisors who molested boys and young men for over twenty years, resulting in the largest criminal investigation into sexual abuse in Canada. Many young men who were molested and abused, all under the symbol of the crucifix, died by suicide. All I know is that we did not sign up for this, and that the Roman Catholic Church lied to hide their many sins in this matter. Many other Native People who went through Catholic residential schools across Canada had similar and even worse stories. Our Native languages and cultures were never appreciated by the white man, and especially not by the Roman Catholic Church. To this day, the Pope has never apologized for the criminal abuses that the clergy have inflicted worldwide. On reflection, I have realized that the Native People meant nothing to the church, and the loss of our good young men was all in vain. And I know the clergy will have to answer to the Creator for this and more.

In the beginning, to get in good with us, the bishops and higher clergy must have directed the priests to learn our languages and to communicate fluently with us in order to gain our trust and parishioners, as a new day was coming for all Native People. The priests became Dene language experts and converted the People to their version of God-made man: Jesus. It was a time of great spiritual confusion. In the Dene way, the Creator is seen in nature and the Creation—you see it in the changes of seasons. The Creator is out in the bush where you can close your eyes and just talk honestly, directly. As boys, when we came out of catechism classes we wondered what the priests were talking about when they told the story of Moses crossing the sea to escape the Pharaoh's army and then wandering for forty years in the desert. Fantastic stuff, but it did not make logical sense—and we were supposed to believe it? Not likely, as many things made no sense to us, but they pushed it as if it came straight from the Voice of Heaven, and there was no discussion as we tried to sort it out in our minds, looking for the truth.

I remember clearly when the Roman Catholic bishop came to our town, by airplane, for his annual visit, and the whole town treated him like a conquering hero. They bowed down to him and kissed his ring. I was ashamed to see my People acting like this, but it didn't seem to bother them, the priests and our Elders busily talking in our language and laughing, while us kids could barely understand what our relatives were saying to us. The moment we entered the residential schools, our language was considered "no good" and we were punished by the nuns for speaking it openly. To me, the bishop's visit was our moment of truth: such hypocrisy in order to collect even more money. Money was their true God.

The Roman Catholic Church won that round. When we left residential school, we felt that we were "damaged goods." We tried to understand the terrible things we had experienced, all in the name of Christianity, as we picked up the broken pieces of ourselves and tried to put them back together, our own personal puzzle. I would not wish it on anyone. The Northwest Territories was poorer for it; many took to drinking to wrestle with the demons that followed us into society and our daily lives. I for one had nightmares and sweats from those days on, trying to rid myself of those lived and seen experiences. Sadly, many never made it, lost and wandering aimlessly in a haze on the streets of our northern towns and cities, killing themselves out in the open in violent and destructive ways, carrying this disease of colonization. The good young men of the North, forever lost to us, and no one knowing what to do. I recognize that I've been hard on the Roman Catholic Church, as they were hard on us, but I also know they had some kind people who listened and helped us when they could.

As I write this, I think of my hometown, Tulita, and of the present situation, in which all the young speak English and only the Elders speak our Dene language, a real break between the generations. It's not only loss of language but, more importantly, loss of traditional knowledge distilled from the Beginning of Time. It is disappearing right in front of us. In my hometown, there was a Mountain Dene leader named Yatsole who gifted our People with fifty-two drum songs that came through dreams, direct from the Creator. The number fifty-two is for the fifty-two weeks of the year; sadly, with the loss of Elders and drummers, we can only remember twenty-nine songs now. It seems the young men are not interested in learning how to hunt and trap and how to live off the land, something we do naturally. They are interested in their computers and iPhones—this after we signed our land claims with the Government of Canada. They expect this settlement will provide for them for life. They don't realize that we need those skills to make this claim work, or we will be forever stuck in neutral, going nowhere fast. I can see that more and more of our songs and our language will be lost. To make matters worse, alcohol and drugs have made serious inroads into our communities and have become part of daily life. Not a bright picture.

This brings me to the other Dene First Nations I've been fortunate to have had the opportunity to meet and work with. In some I see the loss of traditional songs and dances; some cannot even remember their Legends of Creation; some do not even drum anymore. But they all know how to sing *"Ave Maria"*; they all know the hymns from Sunday mass. I will generalize and assume this snapshot is showing us that the cultural loss is *huge* in our Nation in all of the four directions.

I would say to the Elders, leaders and People who are reading this, now is the time to act, to record everything about us—languages, songs, dances, legends, history and so on. We're losing too many of our Elders and our traditional knowledges. We need to use modern technology like video cameras to provide our Nations with cultural and historical records of ourselves to be used in the future. We need to have more of our People writing books, making music, making art, and teaching the history, culture, values and principles of Native Peoples; we need more voices. I would also advise all of the First Nations, Inuit and Métis to start talking with each other about how to save what is left of our cultures. The departments of heritage, culture and education must all work very closely with Native People. Our traditional knowledge, the songs of our unique cultures—these are part of the sacredness that my grandmother told me about when the Creator gifted us with Life and the many gifts to help us succeed in the future. It is up to us as North American Native People to fight for what we are and to reclaim all that we have lost. In that way, we will honour the Creator who gave us Life and our identity.

It is not all doom and gloom. We have come through many dark periods in Canada's history: residential schools, the '60s Scoop, the relocation of Inuit families to the High Arctic, mistreatment of our war veterans, medical experiments on our People in Indian hospitals and so on. The list of sins is long, but we are still here. I want to encourage our People, across our lands, to pound and beat the drums, sing and scream at the top of our voices to the sun and the skies, and invite the spirits of our Ancestors to dance with us as we celebrate ourselves in the lands that were found by our long ago Elders. In a hundred years, we will still be here, as integral parts of Canada, asserting ourselves with pride, making our own trail. I will not be here one hundred years from now, but I will be cheering you on from the side, my People, along with many others. Don't Give Up!

# Strangers in a Not So Strange Land

**DREW HAYDEN TAYLOR**
Playwright & Writer

## THE STORY BEGINS

IT'S GENERALLY BELIEVED THAT WHEN TURTLE ISLAND'S Indigenous population first met Europe's brave, dashing and essentially lost explorers, we were perceived as being a primitive and backwoods people, as we did not use sails, understand metallurgy or believe in draining a country dry of its natural resources. We were odd that way.

Conversely, it was assumed that Indigenous people viewed those same lost White men as god-like, if not gods. Arthur C. Clarke, science fiction author and inventor of the concept of geosynchronous satellites, is famous for saying, "Any sufficiently advanced technology is indistinguishable from magic." That's how they must have appeared: magical and omnipotent. It's theorized that Cortes's conquest of the Aztec empire was made easier by their belief that he was Quetzalcóatl, a returning god.

Personally, I don't view this period of time with such religious iconography. Instead, I view it more as the first alien invasion. The original *War of the Worlds*.

Contrary to popular belief, Indigenous people are no strangers to the concepts of exploring the future or understanding different worlds. Many of our traditional stories are amazingly diverse and fantastic. Weird, even. In fact, those were frequently the best ones told around those collective social and cultural bonfires. Many varied and separate Indigenous nations have ancient stories that are easily familiar to those knowledgeable in the styles of what is often referred to as speculative fiction.

Some examples: There is the Haudenosaunee story of the Seven Dancers. Of course, the details vary slightly among the Six Nations, but essentially it's the tale of seven children who formed a group and decided to dance together, despite advice from adults. So they danced. And danced, always looking upward to the heavens. And as they danced, they began to rise. The parents saw this and called to them to stop and come back, but to no avail. The children kept rising until they became part of the night sky. I'm leaving a lot out, but that is why the Pleiades star cluster is often referred to by the Haudenosaunee as the Seven Dancers. And there is the familiar story of Sky Woman, who fell through a hole in the sky and landed on some geese, who gently placed her on the back of a giant turtle. There, with the help of some accommodating animals, she transformed the turtle's shell into the Earth we all know and love.

Perhaps two of the first examples of a multi-parallel space-time inversion?! Don't you just love those? Or maybe a worm hole. Throw in some terraforming and you've got yourself a pretty cool science fiction tale.

A friend who's very knowledgeable about Anishnawbe legends relayed to me a story he'd been told about Star People. They came from somewhere above and interacted with our ancestors several times. In fact, it was stated, oddly enough, that those visitors were viewed as a very clean and polite people. I think it's interesting to point out that non-Native interactions with Star People have not always been reported to be so courteous. There are no legends among our people regarding anal probes, thank the Creator. That may say more about the settlers than about us or Star People.

Looking at a more popularized example, there are petroglyphs and pictographs. All across Turtle Island and other far-flung countries, ancient peoples have left familiar and not-so-familiar symbols embedded in or decorating rock. Interpretations of these designs are mixed and controversial, but many of the images bear striking similarities to what some believe are astronaut-like and perhaps not of this world.

A cottage industry has even been set up by a sizable number of well-to-do Caucasian experts with way too much time on their hands, who feel Indigenous people of Time Immemorial could not have been responsible for many of our past achievements. Whether it was the pyramids of Central Mexico or our own understanding and mastery of agriculture and irrigation, ancient alien theorists believe we were taught all of this by some of the folks in those images we captured on rocks. If it's brilliant, innovative and clever, something not of this world has to have helped us. It's a fascinating idea but, like many sci-fi tales, a little preposterous.

Not everybody needs a giant black monolith to kickstart their civilizations.

Digging a bit deeper, perhaps one of the best examples of our Ancestors looking to the future is the philosophy of the Seventh Generation. Much like the dreamcatcher, it has become a ubiquitous concept in many teachings and in numerous nations across the country. Essentially it's a belief that every decision we make, every action we take, will have repercussions for the next seven generations. Care and thought must be put into everything we consider, because down the road, it will have a direct impact our grandchildren and their descendants.

Currently, popular thought in Canada has Indigenous people tending to look backward, at what we lost, what we are trying to get back, what we are trying to reinstate. I think that's only part of our understanding. All trails go in two directions. We were a people who also looked forward. A lot of that was lost in the twentieth century, as we did battle with the spectre of colonization, residential schools and the pervasive creep of the dominant culture. It's only recently that we've put our storytelling moccasins on again and are carving out our places around the campfire, where telling our Indigenous tales is not a federal offence.

But thanks to that dominant culture, Indigenous people weren't exactly omitted from future appearances. If you'll pardon the pun, they had just been whitewashed.


## THE STORY CONTINUES

AS A KID growing up on the reserve, I hoovered up television—what I could see on three fuzzy and snowy channels—and practically lived in the school library. With no internet or satellite reception at that time, life could be boring on a small reserve. A young boy needed to find entertainment where he could. There were only so many trees I could climb. So I read and watched everything, especially science fiction. Why I'm not too sure. It could possibly be the fact that a lot of the literature we were exposed to via school—life in sixteenth-century England, or other periods in the dominant culture's history—was far more confusing than what I found coming from the minds of science fiction writers and creators. Interestingly, they were very relatable to this child.

I never really understood the appeal of *The Catcher in the Rye*, but loved *The Chrysalids*. Middle-class white angst was alien (sorry) to us on the Rez, but stories about kids feeling different and afraid about where and how they fit into society—got it. And loved it.

Frequently thought of as the bastard child of legitimate literature, good science fiction can and does accomplish much of what other forms of literary expression do. It explores the human condition. Isn't that what all literature is about? The only difference is that science fiction uses different tools. We Indigenous people know a few things about the human condition. Think of the situation as us culturally appropriating the genre and then Indigenizing it.

Another way of looking at it is that those elements of the future are like a filter through which we can explore our world today. Put some space suits on and carry some laser-beam weapons, and science fiction can still give us something that could apply to our struggles today.

Everybody loves a good metaphor.

And let's face it, what people in North America have a better understanding of a strange, exotic race suddenly showing up out of nowhere with different technology and basically taking everything over? I have it on good authority that it's happened before.

For this little kid, one of the first representations of Indigenous people in the genre of science fiction was a familiar one. I have a feeling it was the same for many North Americans. It came from the journeys of a starship called *Enterprise*. In the original *Star Trek* series, there was an episode in the third season called "The Paradise Syndrome." Simply, the *Enterprise* landing party arrives on a doomed planet populated by Native North Americans, specifically a combination of Delaware, Mohegan and Navaho people. Indigenous people travel halfway across the galaxy and we are still endangered. Sigh.

More interestingly, these three disparate nations—suddenly plopped on a distant planet by aliens however many hundreds of years ago—blend together, resulting in a society of beaded headbands, fringed miniskirts and no knowledge of lamps or sustainable agriculture. Threatened by an approaching asteroid, they do what all Indians did at that time: they waited for a white saviour to rescue them. And this time, his name was Kirk.

As a young Native boy, I remember naïvely thinking how cool this episode was. Any representation was better than no representation. We couldn't live on just *The Beachcombers* episodes. I didn't have enough worldly knowledge to know how wrong this episode was in its depiction, and on so many different levels, too, but at least there were Native people in the future. That was something. Many times in our recent past, even that has looked dubious.

A second *Star Trek* appearance, other than a bizarre animated episode, came in *Star Trek: The Motion Picture.*

In a very short scene, where Kirk is giving a briefing to a sizable portion of his crew in the shuttle bay, there are two shots of three Native people amidst all the other humans and aliens. What's interesting is that everybody is dressed in standard Starfleet uniforms. Except the Indigenous people. Yes, they have the uniforms on, but they, and it seems *only* they, are sporting accessories and cultural affectations. And they stand out noticeably because of it. Recognizably ornate necklaces, feathers, hair ornaments, etcetera. It seems little has changed in three hundred years. I couldn't help wondering if there was a powwow taking place on Ten Forward.

And the less said about *Star Trek: Voyager*'s Chakotay, the better. At the time, Robert Beltran's casting as the frustratingly vague Indigenous first officer was seen as a progressive statement, almost as groundbreaking as creating the first female starship captain. However, I have it on good authority that Kate Mulgrew was actually a woman. Beltran's authenticity as a man of the corn soup/bannock denomination, not so much. I believe he was Mexican-American.

Second in my understanding of the field was a book I came across in high school, titled *Brave New World*, by Aldous Huxley. A tale about an advanced utopian or dystopian (depending on your perspective) future where everybody has what they want and they seem no better off for it. Biology is manipulated via birthing tanks, resulting in segments of the population purposely being given grades of intelligence and ability, as needed by society. And plenty of drugs to keep the population happy.

Somewhere in this future exists what is called the Savage Reservation, an area in the American Southwest free of technology or the dominant culture: "A savage reservation is a place which, owing to unfavorable climatic or geological conditions, or poverty of natural resources, has not been worth the expense of civilizing." It's anathema to the antiseptic, pristine and controlled world most of that civilization lives in. Here the inhabitants give birth in the old-fashioned, ineffectual way, believe in gods, experience sadness and pain, grow old and, in one case, learn an awful lot about Shakespeare.

While specifics are rare regarding a particular Indigenous locale or people, according to Google it's loosely based on the Zuni people. Most of the time, these savages appear to be getting drunk on homemade mescal or flagellating themselves in the hope that their cornfields will get rain. It does not sound like a pleasant place. But speaking as a twenty-first century Aboriginal, at least their water is drinkable.

These are the two options for the future, as presented in the book.

*Star Trek* and *Brave New World* entered my consciousness in my teens. Occasionally there would be other blips on the sci-fi cultural radar but, for the most part, that was the extent of Indigenous people in the future. Neither was particularly encouraging.

Occasionally I would hear about random books like *Svaha*, by non-Native author Charles de Lint: "Out beyond the Enclaves, in the desolation between the cities, an Indian flyer has been downed. A chip encoded with vital secrets is missing. Only Gahzee can venture forth to find it—walking the line between the Dreamtime and the Realtime, bringing his people's ancient magic to bear on the poisoned world of

tomorrow."[1] Sounds like fun. Might be just another week-
end in Curve Lake First Nation, but I could never find a copy
of the book.

And then there was *The Indians Won*, by well-known
mainstream author Martin Cruz Smith, who claims some
Native American heritage. It's a pretty cool alternate universe story about what would have happened if all the
great Indigenous leaders of the late nineteenth century
had banded together to form a practical army and kept
the American nation and people at bay. It takes place in a
present-day reality, and on an Indigenous sovereign nation.
It poses some interesting questions.

Other similar books would pop up occasionally, but
none sufficiently original or brilliant enough to leave a
noticeable mark in the popular cultural zeitgeist. The ideas
needed for a contemporary Indigenous science fiction ren-
aissance lay sleeping.

The vast majority of science fiction books are dire
warnings of future tragic incidents to come. Science fiction,
usually as a rule, presents a gloomy and problematic future.
For example, H.G. Wells's *The Time Machine* and *The Shape
of Things to Come* came up a little short in happy endings.

*Dune*, by Frank Herbert; *Fahrenheit 451* and *The
Martian Chronicles*, both by Ray Bradbury; *Animal Farm*,
by George Orwell; *Starship Troopers*, by Robert E. Heinlein;
*Do Androids Dream of Electric Sheep?* by Philip K. Dick; *The
Handmaid's Tale*, by Margaret Atwood; *Ready Player One*,
by Ernest Cline—and the list could go on. It's the general
consensus that the future will not be a fun place. *Star Wars*

....................

1    Charles de Lint, *Svaha* (New York: Orb Books, 2000).

is considered more of a fantasy fable then hard science fiction, where *2001: A Space Odyssey* is in that grey zone. But no matter how you look at it, every New Year's brings us closer to disaster.

Of course, it's a truism that most if not all drama, in all its many forms, is built on dysfunction and difficulty. Tolstoy wrote, "All happy families are alike; each unhappy family is unhappy in its own way." The same can be said about literature. Off the top of my head, I cannot come up with any futuristic book extolling the virtues of a tomorrow to come. Then again, books about the present and also the past are seldom happy or inspiring. Romance novels not included—even though there's a sub-genre of what is called science fiction romance. And the writing is exactly what you'd think the combining of those two fields would create.

The very nature of novels and storytelling demands that the central character face and overcome a series of obstacles to either achieve or be denied their objective. So disappointment and tragedy are understandably part of the whole storytelling tradition. Sitting around a campfire or shelling out some money to read a book in which there is no difficulty or excitement seems counterproductive. Stories with little hanging in the balance tend to leave you wanting. By nature, as participants in the storytelling journey we demand a certain amount of danger, a literary roller coaster. And the more dysfunctional the world in which the story takes place, the greater the potential catharsis. We are hardwired that way. So even though there may be a happy ending by definition, the environment in which the story takes place seldom changes. Especially in science fiction.

With all that said, Indigenous sci-fi does doesn't have much of a brighter outlook for the future either. It too is grim and unforgiving. That Seventh Generation philosophy does not seem to give the Indigenous people of this country any advantages.

First things first, though: some background on Indigenous literature. I think it's safe to say that in the last forty years there has been a delightful explosion of Native writing in Canada and the United States. Authors like Louise Erdrich, Lee Maracle, Richard Wagamese, Jeannette Armstrong, Katherena Vermette, Tomson Highway, Tracey Lindberg, Leslie Marmon Silko, Beatrice Mosionier and Tom King, to name just a few, have all made impressive contributions to this new subgenre. Their specialization might be Indigenous but their impact is worldwide. Poetry, novels, plays, non-fiction, film are all now flying the flag of Indigenous colonization—we are culturally appropriating the literary arts.

These publications, told from the perspective of a once persecuted people, voice stories about the way things were, and are. Usually angry and tragic, they've frequently been referred to as trauma porn, focusing on the repercussions of colonization. As I said earlier, happy stories about successful and stable Indigenous people prospering in the dominant culture have been few and far between. A lot of psychological and oppressive demons were being exorcised. Much of it was a form of cathartic writing.

The birth of present-day Indigenous science fiction was actually quite recent. In fact, in the last decade or so there has been a veritable flood of stories by and featuring Indigenous people, all exploring the journey into the future. So it should be no surprise that the transition to stories about the years to come would also bear that legacy of dark foreboding. What's additionally fascinating is the wide breadth of topics and issues explored within its covers—cultural survival, environmentalism, LGBT concerns and so on.

For the sake of brevity, I'm going to mention a few select books and a play that have been published in the last ten or so years (not all, or my contribution to this volume would be book length in itself). Most have been successful and popular, shedding new light on concerns now being discussed in our communities. These are interesting times.

### Moon of the Crusted Snow, Waubgeshig Rice

An amazing story about a northern Ontario reserve in the aftermath of a power outage, cutting it off permanently from the rest of the world. Rich in detail and character, it contemplates how a First Nation grown reliant on the tools of civilization would survive if forced to rely on its ancestral heritage. There's not a lot of hard science mentioned in the writing, so its inclusion here might be questioned. It also happens in the present, and some might feel it falls more into the fantasy universe. But put next to many of the genre's best apocalyptic tales, it holds up quite well, because like all good stories, sci-fi or otherwise, it makes you wonder what you would do in the same situation. Rumour has it that Rice is working on a sequel.

### The Unplugging, Yvette Nolan

In the same vein as *Moon of the Crusted Snow*, though taking place a few decades down the road, the play *The Unplugging* also explores the repercussions of life in a world where the electrical grid has gone down and society must find a way to survive. Two women, forced out of one of the last bastions of civilization, must rely on traditional wisdom to survive in the wilderness, proving they alone might possess the tools for the world's continued existence. It's an interesting exploration of how some of the evils of the past, like sexism, if given a chance will find a way to prosper in a brutal environment. So will bravery and perseverance.

*The Marrow Thieves*, Cherie Dimaline

Winner of the 2017 Governor General's Literary Award for Young People's Literature, Dimaline's story sets up a world where Indigenous people are being hunted by government and corporate forces. The dominant culture can no longer dream, which has led to widespread madness. The only cure: the harvesting of DNA from the bones of the few remaining First Nations people who still have the ability to dream. An unfortunate by-product of the harvesting—death. As seen through the eyes of a fifteen-year-old boy on the run, dodging professional hunters, it's a bleak look into the future. One of those novels for younger audiences that adults can also enjoy.

*Love Beyond Body, Space and Time: An Indigenous LGBT Sci-Fi Anthology*, Hope Nicholson (editor)

Most unique in this assortment, this anthology is advertised as a collection of Indigenous science fiction and urban fantasy focusing on LGBT and two-spirited characters. A slim but powerful book, it includes such writers as Richard

Van Camp, Cherie Dimaline and Daniel Heath Justice, just to name a few, all pushing the space age envelope, boldly taking us where so few have gone before. The compilation shows how truly far this genre has come, and how inclusive it's become, in so few years. Much like Dimaline's book for young audiences, this does not have to be enjoyed by just the LGBT community.

*Moonshot*, Hope Nicholson and Elizabeth LaPensée (editors)

This is an amazing sci-fi graphic novel series highlighting original works by Canadian and American Indigenous authors who have a more exotic imagination. Richard Van Camp, Jay Odjick and Jennifer Storm are just three of those whose visions run rampant every two years. Visually bold, narratively exciting, there are currently three volumes, with another one eagerly anticipated.

*Take Us to Your Chief and Other Stories*

At the risk of promoting my own agenda, there's my own book on the subject. It's a collection of my short stories. I wanted to pay homage to the tropes of the classic science fiction stories I grew up with and learned to love. These tales explore such fundamental aspects of the genre as artificial intelligence, time travel, aliens landing, space travel, government conspiracies and so on, all encased in familiar Indigenous surroundings. With a generous helping of humour. It was so much fun to write.

*Trail of Lightning*, Rebecca Roanhorse

I'd heard about this book even before it was published. Coming from south of the border, and bursting onto the speculative fiction/fantasy scene, Roanhorse's unique book is a combination of sci-fi, romance, fantasy, mystery, and traditional teachings. After a global environmental apocalypse, times have changed on the Navaho Reservation. Navaho monsters and gods once again roam the land, and Maggie, a monster hunter, must make sense of a young girl's disappearance. And how's this for a vote of confidence: Roanhorse was asked to write a novel, *Resistance Reborn*, for the Star Wars universe. Okay, I'm jealous.

THIS IS JUST the proverbial tip of the literary iceberg. Writers like Jennifer Givhan, Daniel H. Wilson and Stephen Graham Jones have all made great contributions to the field. Also, if you want a more in-depth exploration of the topic, Grace Dillon's study of the genre, titled *Walking the Clouds: An Anthology of Indigenous Science Fiction*, is amazing. She deconstructs Indigenous writing from North America, Australia and New Zealand. Talk about your dream job.

And let's not forget the cinema, where the film *Blood Quantum*, written and directed by Jeff Barnaby, gave zombie movies a different, political perspective. The usual undead apocalypse hits the land, people running and screaming, and the only survivors are Indigenous people living on a Mi'kmaq reserve, who have an immunity to the virus. A discussion on who has enough Indigenous blood to be allowed on the reserve begins. Factions develop and chaos ensues. Clever and innovative.

Oddly enough, if we cast our nets further afield, the Maori of Aotearoa have made some interesting appearances as characters in films highlighting the amazing. *Virus* featured Donald Sutherland, Jamie Lee Curtis and Maori actor Cliff Curtis (no relation to Jamie) doing battle with an aggressive alien intelligence that has taken control of a science vessel at sea. There's even a fearsome haka as Cliff Curtis tries to intimidate an ad hoc robot, made by the intelligence, menacingly waving a Maori jade club. (Spoiler alert—he loses.)

Sometime earlier, in 1985 to be specific, the New Zealand film, *The Quiet Earth*, featured Maori Pete Smith as one of the only three survivors of a worldwide apocalypse resulting from a scientific experiment gone awry. As they try to figure out what to do, a love triangle develops and the usual hijinks occur.

Frequently a marker of pop culture interest, Marvel comics has released several issues involving First Nations heroes, including a member of the X-Men. Decades ago, in order to add non-white characters, the cartoon series *Super Friends* created Apache Chief, who had the ability to grow to fifty feet by uttering the phrase "Inuk chuk," which is thought to originate from the Inuit word *Inuksuk*. Too much wrong with that whole sentence to get into right now, but suffice it to say, while all the other Super Friends were dressed up in cool, ultramodern clothing, Apache Chief wore the usual stereotypical headband, bare-chested except for a plain vest, and the ubiquitous breechcloth. As can be expected, he spoke in stereotypical "Indian" fashion, frequently spouting native American pseudo-philosophy.

But perhaps most representative of the dawning of a new age in terms of Indigenous representation in the future, Artificial Intelligence and video games. Storytelling among our people began orally. And as the colonizer took hold on the land, the telling of stories gradually evolved into theatre, print, radio, television, movies and so on, to the point where many video games now have intricate and detailed narratives to entice the participant.

At the forefront of this is Elizabeth LaPensée, an Anishinaabe, Métis and Irish professor in the departments of Media and Information and Writing, Rhetoric and American Cultures at Michigan State University. Her award-winning games and art teach stories and history, but also help contextualize modern Indigenous life, especially online. She even offers a game-writing workshop called Indigenous Futurisms in Games, which she described to me this way:

Delve into game design and writing through the lens of Indigenous Futurisms, which reflects past, present, and future. You will adapt your ideas into game mechanics and plan out design for your own game. Hands-on experience will contribute to skills in how to integrate story with gameplay including approaches ranging from environmental storytelling to pitching as you build towards a conceptual proto-type that you can continue to work on.

A lot of this is way over my head, but it does show how our storytellers are preparing and able to face what the future may throw at us.

For those interested in all forms of Indigenous futurisms, there is a festival called IndigiPop X, essentially an Indigenous Comicon, taking place annually in

Albuquerque, New Mexico. There, as many as two thousand other IndigiNerds participate in panels, attend workshops, and generally revel in the amazing world of science fiction, fantasy and horror. I guess you could say birds of a feather—and, no, that is not an Indigenous aphorism.

Science fiction, by its very nature, asks us to believe what could be, not what is. Maybe that's why it's become so popular in First Nations cultures. Most of it shows us as survivors, regardless of what's happening.

I've always had faith in the Seventh Generation.

And as a sci-fi icon is known to say, make it so.

THE STORY ENDS

# Me Tomorrow: The Journey Begins . . .

**TAE:HOWĘHS, AKA AMOS KEY JR.**
**A ROYAL MOHAWK**
Educator & Advocate

## THE CANADIAN INDIGENOUS CONTEXT

ELLO, READER. MY SPIRIT NAME IS TAE:HOWĘHS ("HE works with words"). This name descends from the Turtle Clan of my mother. As per custom, I had no choice in this matter.

I was born in the United States, and I had no choice over that either. I am a staunch Mohawk of the Haudenosaunee Confederacy and a Citizen of the Q:gwehǫ:weh Civilization on Turtle Island, which makes up both Canada and the United States. A seasoned science teacher once said to me, "Your people are right: the North American plate is actually floating on molten rock and, yes, it's actually an island." This explanation works for me, even when using the metaphor of an island shaped like a Turtle. If North America were not an island, many of its coastal cities would be underwater: New York City would sit 1,427 feet under the Atlantic, Boston 1,823 feet under, and Miami 2,410 feet

under; New rleans would be 2,416 feet below the surface
of the Gulf of Mexico, and Los Angeles would be 3,756 feet
below the surface of the Pacific. Do the math: how did our
ancestors know this?

Spiritual Leaders from the Q:gwehǫ:weh Civilization
known as Faith Keepers bestowed my name, Tae:howęhs,
in ceremony on behalf of the Creator, in front of hundreds
gathered at the Seneca Longhouse at Six Nations of Grand
River, in southern ntario many, many, many winters ago.
I was a mere infant at the time, swaddled in the love of my
people and the smiles of all those who looked on. My name
was raised with songs from the Canon of Special Songs for
our Creator, whom we call Adǫwa. It was hoped from that
day forward that my Creator would use that name to call
and address me. This name will be especially important
when the time comes and he calls me back home, saying
"You have been there long enough!" I will then journey home
to be with all my family members and ancestors who have
returned home ahead of me: tsę ni yǫ gao sǫ gi hę dęs.

In the mid-1980s, I was elevated to the Circle of Faith
Keepers of the Longhouse. Again, I had no choice about
being elevated to this Circle. I fought being considered
to join this Circle because I had been away at college and
university, and after teaching for the London Board of Education, I had lost a good amount of my proficiency in my
first language, simply because I had no one to talk to, every
day, in my language.

Not accepting this elevated designation caused such a
commotion among the Elders and other Faith Keepers that
they held meetings and found a way to speak to my heart.
They explained to me in the eloquent prose of our Cayuga
language that our birth and journey in life is preordained

by the Shǫgwayadisǫh, our Creator. After much emotion and sage advice, I finally accepted. The Ceremony of Investiture, inducting me into the Circle of Faith Keepers, went on as planned, in front of all the Longhouse People gathered for our Green Corn Ceremonies. It is at such high ceremonies that these auspicious yet humbling occasions occur. My parents, siblings and extended family were so proud, and I was humbled to tears. I will carry that designation now to my grave and back home to be with Shǫgwayadisǫh, our Creator. I have since worked at becoming more proficient in my language, so I now speak, dream, laugh and sing in the Cayuga Language. I now understand the benefits of being truly bilingual. Being bilingual has afforded me certain privileges. As a result of being bilingual, I have grown comfortable steeped in two ideologies, two societies, two sensibilities, two intelligences and with two names, just to name a few.

## OUR HAUDENOSAUNEE GENESIS

OUR GENESIS TELLS us we are Sky People, the Ǫ:gwehǫ:weh. It is nice to read and hear that science is just now catching up with our Genesis through their big bang theory.

I am so glad that words such as *death*, *dead* and *died* are insults in our languages. We can say those words in our languages too, but it demeans the person's stature. We prefer instead the phrases Aǫdawihshęh (they are resting now) or Asǫngihędęhs (they went on ahead of us). These phrases, emanating from our Cayuga Language, are so beautiful. They tell us that in our transcendence, the moment we return to the Sky World, or O:węja ǫweh, we will move along a path covered in strawberries, with the air saturated with their aroma. As we creep ever closer to our home in the Sky World, we will hear the music of the Great Feather Dance, the O:stowah Gowah, rendered in our honour!

We are told that we will be greeted by a long line of grandparents, uncles and aunties, our mother and father and our siblings, who happen to have gone home ahead of us, back to the Sky World. It is then that we, our relatives and our Clan, can join the throngs of jubilant Q:gwehǫ:weh people and join the O:stowah Gowah, the Great Feather Dance of our Creator, rendered in both of our honours. We will be home together forever, to enjoy the euphoria of His Ho:dęnidǫshra, His altruism, His benevolence and His love.

So it is, with these teachings and ways of knowing as a backdrop, and armed with His magnificent Ho:dęnidǫshra and the noble tenets carried by my Relatives, Clan, Faith Keepers and the Four Holy Guardians, which inform my Indigeneity and give agency to my Q:gwehǫ:weh Civiliz-ation, that I will now share with the next generations my thoughts as points to ponder for *Me Tomorrow*.

I am always learning. And as each winter and sum-mer passes, I learn that much more—it's like cognitive psychology and EQ-i (emotional quotient inventory) con-verging and intersecting at the same time. It can be fun, discovering and rationalizing these "aha" moments.

I write at this moment to make suggestions for future consideration so that as Indigenous Peoples, settlers and Canadians we can become more civilized and humane, both as a people and as a country. Perhaps we can work on these suggestions as "points to ponder" over the next fifty to seventy-five years. I will not get to see these points to ponder evolve with you, as I will be Dancing in the Sky with my Sky People. While there, I will continue to sing, dance and ponder, perhaps during and after a heavenly and succulent dinner of roast venison, roasted potatoes and mushrooms, and some of the tasty aged nectar of our harvest. Mmmm, good.

The following "Me Tomorrows" are presented in no particular order of importance, as they are all important to consider. Here we go . . .

## AMENDING THE CONSTITUTION OF CANADA: A REBIRTH

IN THE ME TOMORROW:

Canada will attempt to and make strides toward becoming more civilized. It will "open up" the Canadian Constitution and finally adopt the "distinct society" status of Quebec, so Quebec will feel comfortable endorsing and adopting it.

In this Canadian moment, Indigenous Civilizations in Canada will be able to exert their Indigenous agency, allowing their role in the country to change and evolve. This will create a modern-day reckoning. These Indigenous Civilizations will use their cunning and collective intelligence to articulate their Agency, Moral Compass, Moral Imperatives and Moral Authority. These Indigenous Civilizations will now insist on being included in the rewriting of the Canadian Constitution.

Moving forward, citizens of Indigenous Civilizations will be armed with the inalienable human rights that most Canadians enjoy (Canadian human rights were not conferred upon Indigenous Peoples by the Canadian Human Rights Commission until June 2011). Our Indigenous Agency will be supported by the Truth and Reconciliation Commission's 94 Calls to Action from December 2015 and the United Nations Declaration on the Rights of Indigenous Peoples (UNDRIP) passed in September 2007 (by 144 votes, with Canada voting against its adoption). Canada finally adopted UNDRIP in May 2016, paving the road into Canadian law with Royal Assent in June 2021 as Bill C-15. These Indigenous Rights are now adopted by nearly all countries in the world who are seeking to become more civilized.

In the future, the privileged French and English in Canada, along with the Supreme Court of Canada, will realize that the French and English are not the only founding nations in Canada.

As Canada becomes more just and civilized, the next generations will realize the truths of their own Ancestors and that of their Canadian/Eurocentric Civilization and privilege. They will realize that Canada previously has made Indigenous Civilizations outcasts in their own country—sort of elephants in the room. The courts and the United Nations will determine that Indigenous Civilizations and their Nations are also founding nations of Canada. The French and English will soon realize that they as peoples only differ because of their linguistic differences and a few lingering customs transposed from their original homelands in Europe.

Canada will amend the Canadian Constitution to include all of the sixty-plus Indigenous Civilizations and their legal Nations in Canada as founding nations and co-stewards of the Land. All sixty-plus Indigenous

Civilizations and their Nations will then have equal and legal standing in the Constitution of Canada.

The UNDRIP will have legal standing in Canada and will be a companion document to the new Canadian Constitution, much like the Charter of Rights and Freedoms exists today.

The new Constitution of Canada will affirm in its preamble that it will adopt the name *Gayę'shra Gowah* (the Great Law), borrowing from one of the world's first and original constitutions of the world, that of the Haudenosaunee Civilization and their democracy. It has to be remembered that when the rest of the world was being led by kings and queens, the Haudenosaunee and the Anishinaabe had already developed highly sophisticated and evolved democracies. These democracies were so peace-loving that they evolved without militias or armies. These two democracies were known as the Five Nations Confederacy of the Haudenosaunee and the Three Fires Confederacy of the Anishinaabe.

Section 35 of the current Constitution of Canada, which "recognizes and affirms Aboriginal rights," is all but a footnote, an afterthought, and will no longer need to exist once the amendments of the new constitution are ratified.

The Mothers and Fathers of this new constitution will realize that they no longer need the Royal Family as head of state as well.

Each of the sixty-plus Indigenous Civilizations, the Métis and the Inuit will appoint de facto members to Parliament and/or the Senate, and the provinces and territories will in turn appoint or elect an equal number of Parliamentarians and Senators as per custom.

## ABOLISHING THE SINISTER AND RACIST INDIAN ACT

IN THE ME TOMORROW:

In line with the new Canadian Constitution, the racist Indian Act will be abolished. In its place, the Indigenous Civilizations of Canada will each craft their own constitutions in each province and territory. All First Nations communities will craft individual charters of rights and freedoms that are empowered by the respective Indigenous Constitutions of their Civilizations. For instance, Ontario will have three constitutions: one for the Mushkegowuk/Cree; one for the Anishinaabeg/Three Fires Confederacy; and one for the Q:gwehǫ:weh/Six Nations Confederacy. In addition, the Tyendinega Mohawks, Ahkwesasne Mohawks, Wahta Mohawks, Six Nations of Grand River and Oneida of the Thames will first create a modern-day written constitution for their Haudenosaunee Civilization, with the core values and principles of the Great Law. In turn, each Nation will write their own charters of rights and freedoms based on their need to uphold the overarching Haudenosaunee Constitution. In short, it will be stated that the rights and freedoms of the Great Law will not be derogated or abrogated.

This will replace Canada's Indian Act, the most racist piece of legislation ever written in the world. Have you ever heard of a French Act, a Jewish Act, a Chinese Act or an Irish Act?

## OFFICIAL LANGUAGES OF CANADA

IN THE ME TOMORROW:

The official languages of Canada will include the more than seventy Indigenous languages of the Indigenous Civilizations of Canada. Don't be shocked. If India, a former Commonwealth nation like Canada, can officially recognize twenty-two languages, wherein over one hundred are spoken, surely Canada can recognize the more than seventy Indigenous languages in Canada, plus French and English.

Bill C-91, An Act Respecting Indigenous languages, will evolve to the level and standing of the Official Languages Act. Like the Official Languages Act, which was substantially rewritten in 1988, Bill C-91 may have to be rewritten at a future date to include language rights and the rights of Indigenous People to be educated in their languages, with ancillary financial resourcing. The Commissioner of Indigenous Languages will have the authority to hear appeals and will enact policy for an arbitration mechanism to remedy these appeals that the original Bill C-91 did not include. The Office of Indigenous Languages will be expanded to appoint three Language Commissioners, one each for the Métis, Inuit and First Nations, so as to honour each of the Aboriginal Groups cited in the Constitution of Canada, 1982.

## THE DEPARTMENT OF MOTHER EARTH

IN THE ME TOMORROW:

The New Canada will have a Federal Department of Mother Earth, established through an Act of Parliament:

Bill 01, An Act respecting the Rights of Mother Earth. This law will provide oversight of the stewarding of lands, extraction of resources, and water security in Canada, mirroring similar legislation in New Zealand and Bolivia.

Can you imagine?

## EXISTING NUMBERED TREATIES WILL BE AMENDED

IN THE ME TOMORROW:

The existing numbered treaties in Canada will get a rethink with new legislation. As the new modern-day constitutions of Indigenous Civilizations come into force, their preambles will affirm and confirm the existence of their numbered treaty and will state that the numbered treaty will not be abrogated, nor derogated. This will also allow for a new formula and process for writing new treaties and amending the numbered treaties with Canada. New treaties will have the force of the original treaties set out with the Crown, but will also affirm languages, confirm membership and statehoods, and include an amendment process and mechanism. The new legislation will establish a schedule for review and a process to keep the numbered treaties in Canada always "au courant" and "living." This process will keep treaties in line with new developments, realities, laws, rights and sensibilities. A comprehensive appeals process and tribunal will also be established to provide oversight and dispense remedies. And so on . . . This action will restore the tarnished lustre and honour of the Crown in the eyes of Indigenous Peoples in Canada.

## RESOURCE DEVELOPMENT AND TAXATION

IN THE ME TOMORROW:

Tax practices will finally include Indigenous Civilizations and their First Nations. Each Indigenous Civilization in the new Canadian Constitution will set up a taxation process and fee structure that is equal to those of the provincial and territorial governments. One-third of the taxation regime will be delegated to the local First Nations. The provincial and the federal governments will use the other two shares for their goods and services tax, sales tax, resource extraction and excise taxes, business development taxes and so on. The full geographical expanse of the existing treaty area will be considered in determining the tax entitlements of the provincial and federal governments and the Treaty Nations. Each First Nations community will enjoy and invest their third of the taxes collected in any way they choose.

## PROVINCIAL AND TERRITORIAL ACADEMIC INSTITUTIONS AND COLLEGES

IN THE ME TOMORROW:

Indigenous Civilizations and populations in Canada need a reset. We need and deserve a "critical mass" of competent Indigenous leaders possessing values and principles based in their Indigeneity, and wielding both a humble confidence and a degree of audacity. We also need a critical mass of Indigenous scholars, academics and social innovators. And we must develop, examine and understand an Indigenous "index of well-being" and a set of Indigenous social and health determinants and indices.

When I was a student, I was never asked by my guidance counsellor, "Might you want to become a professor, an academic or a scholar?" That was not on our Indigenous radar. Further, I was never told the salary range of a professor. It is quite handsome, I can tell you. It was not until much later, when I joined the University of Toronto, that I began to understand this world and its opportunities. With that experience, I will share my hope for the future of our younger and next generations.

## INDIGENOUS ACADEMIC INSTITUTIONS

IN THE ME TOMORROW:
Each province and territory will have an Indigenous academic institution, a university or college fully funded by each province or territory for each of the Indigenous Civilizations residing there. For example, there will be five Indigenous universities in Ontario, one for each of the Mushkegowuk, Aanishinaabe, Qgwehǫweh Métis and Inuit. Each province will also develop an Indigenous Council of Quality Assurance to approve the standards for Indigenous degrees and courses. (In Ontario, currently, I cannot identify one Indigenous scholar/academic on the provincial Quality Assurance Council.)

The Indigenous universities will have co-op and co-major experiential degrees at the bachelor's, master's and PhD levels across mainstream departments and faculties. Indigenous community colleges will have the same for diplomas and micro-credentials. Each of these institutions will have undertaken "cluster hires" of Indigenous academics and scholars as required for each department and faculty. Each university will have developed degrees and courses based on Indigeneity or Indigenous ideologies in the province and territory where they reside. Each university will "curate" Indigenous undergrads who will stay at the university of their choice to study at the master's and PhD levels, so as to develop and curate a critical mass of Indigenous scholars and academics in Canada.

Each Indigenous university will have a Centre or Institute of Excellence for Indigenous Governance, Indigenous Civil Service and Indigenous Social Innovation.

Each Indigenous university will have Indigenous co-op/co-major degrees representative of the disciplines and intelligence of their civilizations. This will include a co-op/co-major degree in "Caucasian Studies" so as to fully understand the mindset, aspirations, spirituality and theology of Caucasian Civilizations that settled in North America and around the world. All these degrees will include paid placements in urban and rural Indigenous governments and their agencies.

Each Indigenous university will have Indigenous student residences, based on the sensibilities of the host Indigenous Civilizations, including food and catering services reflecting their Indigenous diets and culinary arts. These residences will also have ancillary student services, study hubs/labs, public performances, feasting, coffee house and gifting spaces, and an arts centre and arts gallery.

Each Indigenous university will examine, validate and credential Indigenous research methods, Indigenous ways of knowing and Indigenous oral traditions.

Each Indigenous university will have cross-faculty courses for co-majors and cross-appointments between faculties.

Each Indigenous university will Indigenize mainstream co-op/co-major courses across faculties, such as Indigenous philosophies, Indigenous psychology and Indigenous principles and core values.

Each Indigenous university will have a centre for applied research and practice in Indigenous polysynthetic languages.

Each Indigenous university will research predominant social disorders that have plagued Indigenous Communities: Acquired Colonization Syndrome and Acquired Q̇:gwehǫ:weh Deficiency Syndrome.[1]

Each Indigenous university will approach Indigenous research and applied research from a position or through a lens of living sociology rather than anthropology.

## A LITERARY AND PERFORMING ARTS IN CANADA

IN THE ME TOMORROW:

An Indigenous Arts Council will be established by order in council, with annual funding from the federal Treasury Board to support Indigenous performing (dance, theatre, music) and literary (poetry, fiction, non-fiction and other forms) arts and cinema (documentary and feature films).

...................

1    Replace "*Q̇:gwehǫ:weh*" with the name of the relevant Indigenous Civilization for this syndrome.

The Indigenous Arts Council will fully fund a national Indigenous arts co-op management course, partnering with diploma- or degree-granting Indigenous institutions.

A National Indigenous Performing and Literary Arts Centre will be established in southern Ontario, called The Northern Thunder (TNT). It will be Canada's first such facility wholly managed by an Indigenous CEO and Indigenous arts managers and artists. It will include a full state-of-the-art proscenium theatre (with fly towers); front- and back-of-house facilities; green rooms; construction shops for sets and costumes; spaces for writing residencies, workshopping and rehearsals; conference space and board-rooms; a cafeteria and a fine dining restaurant to promote Canadian Indigenous culinary arts; and a living arts gallery and a living outdoor amphitheatre and arts plaza.

## WAS THE RELATIONSHIP DEMOCIDE, POLITICIDE, GENOCIDE OR INDIGECIDE?

IN THE ME TOMORROW:

Indigenous Civilizations, scholars, academics and institutions will examine the privileged, unbalanced and unhealthy relationship between European settler and Indigenous Civilizations since the time of Confederation. They will determine if this privileged relationship was state-sponsored Democide, Politicide, Genocide or Indige-cide, Indigecide being the covert, systemic ethnic cleansing of Indigenous Civilizations in Canada, including internment and incarceration on tiny pieces of real estate called Indian reserves; the forced conversion of Indigenous Peoples prac-tising Indigenous theologies and spiritualities via shame, persecution, ridicule and stigma; the indecent assault on Indigenous Human Rights; and the Canadian state–enacted legislation to legalize the criminalization of Indigenous Peoples under the Indian Act to outlaw their languages, music, dance, social systems, core values, ethics, virtues, religious practices and forms of government.

## ME TOMORROW: ONE STEP AT A TIME

I HOPE I will witness some of our Indigenous people crossing some of these roads and bridges on their journey before it is my turn to turn and go back Home to dance with my Sky Relatives and Sky People.

The Me Tomorrow will require many of us to join forces, and to discuss and make these ideas and hopes a reality.

The Me Tomorrow will require allies (some might say accomplices) of all nationalities, stripes, creeds and walks of life to be audacious and confident.

The Me Tomorrow requires all of us to adopt new thinking and to debunk colonial definitions and colonized understandings of Indigenous Culture or Indigenous Cultures, so we can begin to create a paradigm shift leading to the recognition of Indigenous Civilizations—which have always been here. Then we will become the architects of our destiny for a Me Tomorrow.

The Me Tomorrow requires all of us to dream and to begin our journey toward Indigenous emancipation—one step at a time.

Da:netoh—that is all for now.

# Waanishkow (Rising)

**TRACIE LÉOST**
Leader, Activist & Athlete

I COME FROM THE FLOWER BEADWORK PEOPLE IN TREATY 1 territory, the heart and homeland of the Métis Nation. At times, we are referred to as the forgotten people—but we won't be forgotten for much longer, of this I am certain. Indigenous people make up the youngest and fastest growing demographic in the country. We are quite literally the future, and our youth are a powerful and relentless force to be reckoned with.

Seven generations of my family have grown up on the same plot of land in our community. My grandparents still live there, and their home always has the door open for daily visits from their children, grandchildren, great-grandchildren, neighbours and community members. On this land, our identity was established, practised, taken and reclaimed. It is an incredibly powerful feeling to know we survived genocide—on the very same land as they tried to erase us on. Though it should have never been that way, it forced us to be resilient. My Kokum remembers growing up on that land, knowing she was a "half breed" but that it was not a good thing; she never asked questions. Despite the shame associated with being Indigenous, my Kokum hung on to everything she could. Because of her resilience every day throughout the years, her grandchildren and great-grandchildren are proudly Indigenous. She raised her grandbabies and great-grandbabies in our culture. Some of us know how to play the fiddle and jig, some of us are learning our language and making our traditional foods, and others are still hunting and trapping traditionally in our community. It has been a beautiful journey to grow out of the shame my family felt to being lifted up as our generations blend together, reclaiming our identities and practising our culture. We spend our winters together on the lake, setting nets and ice fishing. Four generations of our family are usually on the lake, fishing the way our ancestors did. My grandpa, uncle and cousins taught me how to drive the Bombardier, how to set nets, how to find the jigger simply by listening for its knock and how to fillet pickerel. It is deeply powerful to be on this land, to know all that has happened and to still be here, proudly.

In 2014, I competed in track and field at the North American Indigenous Games in Regina, Saskatchewan. This was the first time my athletic abilities and culture were brought together to be celebrated. I medalled in three out of my four events and came home with a fire burning in me to reconnect with that feeling. Soon after, my activism began—in my Kokum's front yard, the same yard where seven generations of us grew up, where our legacy lies. It started with the Missing and Murdered Indigenous Women (MMIW) Journey of Hope, a 115-kilometre run I did in four days to raise money for and awareness of missing and murdered Indigenous women, girls and two-spirit people (MMIWG2S).

The MMIW Journey of Hope was just the first step. I continued to speak about MMIWG2S on a global plat- form and began spending time in classrooms with youth and the community, sharing my story and learning the stories of others. I was, and continue to be, committed to creating space for Indigenous young people to be safe while reclaiming and creating their identity. Recently, I founded a non-profit called Waanishka Movement Inc., to create safe space for and support the rise of Indigenous young people. We are committed to meeting young ones where they are at and holding space for their unique needs, creating the same space and platform as I once searched for. I have continued to stay connected with sports by coaching in a hockey league that removes the financial barriers associated with participating in sport and recreation. For the last five years, my greatest joy has been spending Tuesday nights at the outdoor rink, coaching and playing hockey with youth. In my family, we take care of each other, so it makes sense that my activism has always been centred in my commun- ity and our sense of peoplehood. Taking care of each other is all I have ever known; it is the responsibility I was gifted in ceremony.

In the Seven Sacred Teachings, the Wolf is the teach- ing of humility. In keeping with the Wolf teaching, I struggle to find the words to speak about my own achievements, not because I do not see them as important, but rather because I care so deeply about my community and honouring them instead of myself while continuing to do the work that needs to be done. At the same time, I sometimes struggle to find enough words, or the right words, to describe my motivation for activism when really it's simple: my "why" will always be fuelled by the immense love I have for my people and my community, by my wanting more for them, wanting everything they have always deserved. In my journey this far, people have told me I would never reach the levels that I have already surpassed. They doubted me and labelled me as their stereotypical lazy, incapable Indian. I wanted to prove that my people deserve more, and I deserve more. Who said that I cannot have a strong sense of self, a deep connection to my identity and a presence in my community and culture, that I cannot be educated in our traditional ways of knowing—all while working toward my university degree, continuing to shatter the glass ceiling and fight for my people? I have been humbled to be granted such distinctions as an Indspire Award, the highest honour bestowed on Indigenous people, for Métis Youth, and to be inducted into the Order of Gabriel Dumont, the highest civil honour among in the Métis Nation—before turning twenty-two. But it will never be about me. It will always be about my community and my people. I always have the immense privilege of bringing those honours back to my community, to our Elders and our youth—where they have always belonged.

I get goosebumps when I think about Indigenous young people. I am reminded of the Iroquois Seven Generations teaching of stewardship, a concept that reminds the current generations to work in a sustainable manner to ensure a positive future for the following seven generations. Specifically, in the Métis Nation, when we understand our historical experience, we have gone through seven different phases: the Founders, the Proud Nation, the Defeated Nation, the Shamed Nation, the

Hidden Nation, the Lost Nation and now the Found Nation. The idea of these seven phases comes from Rosie[1] and the Truth and Reconciliation Commission. The explanation of them comes from my own understanding of the history of my Nation, taught to me by my community, Elders, Knowledge Keepers and teachers.

The Founders were the generation that birthed our Nation. The voyageurs (European men—French, English or Scottish) came to the Prairies with the North West Company and Hudson's Bay Company as fur traders. The fur trade was dependent on First Nations communities. Along the way, voyageurs began to have relationships with First Nations women; their children were a mix of European and First Nations ancestry, and thus a distinct Nation and culture was born.

As the fur trade continued and the Founders had children, the Proud Nation lived with its own distinct culture and peoplehood, able to flow perfectly between both worlds, between colonialism and traditions, while also forming their own sense of identity.

The Defeated Nation were the children of the Proud Nation. Growing up with pride in their culture and peoplehood, the Defeated Nation fought for our rights. Often left out and excluded from decision making—for example, when the Crown signed the treaties with First Nations but not the Métis—the Defeated Nation fought for rights that acknowledged and suited the needs of the Métis. The most famous people from the Defeated Nation were Louis Riel

. . . . . . . . . . . . . . . . . .

1    *Rosie on Reconciliation*, National Centre for Truth and Reconciliation, September 30, 2020. https://www.facebook.com/watch/?v=665559731065749.

and Gabriel Dumont, with their Provisional Government. When the Crown came to survey the land of Métis families to transfer to European newcomers, Louis Riel and a handful of Métis men stepped on the chain of the surveyor and demanded that the land transfer be stopped. Louis Riel, now known as the Father of Manitoba, became the leader of the Métis Nation, fighting for Métis rights and distinguishing Manitoba as a province. The Métis Nation succeeded in many battles, furthering our strength as a Nation. The Northwest Resistance was a result of First Nations and Métis anger with the Canadian government for going against the agreements they had made and continuing their expansion into the Prairies and Western Canada. Support by Indigenous matriarchs was crucial during the resistance, a note that is often overlooked in the history books. The Métis and surrounding First Nations gave everything they had to fighting for their rights and were left with nothing. The Métis were dispossessed of the land they occupied and the scrip they were entitled to. Louis Riel was hanged in Regina, and eight Cree warriors were hanged in North Battleford, Saskatchewan, the largest mass hanging in Canadian history.

This defeat led to the Shamed Nation. The Shamed Nation grew up struggling with their identity and extremely poor. They were pushed out of the towns where they lived or the surrounding homestead areas, and were forced to live on road allowances, sections of Crown-owned land located on "the wrong side of the tracks."

Then came the Hidden Nation. Being known to be a "half breed" wasn't a good thing, and if you could pass as white it was best to hide your Indigenous identity. This meant leaving language, culture and traditions behind in order to survive. Métis cultural and traditional practices were illegal. Métis children attending school were singled out and humiliated, and they never fully fit in to either world—too brown for the white kids and too white for the brown kids.

With the Hidden Nation having suppressed their identity to survive, the children of the Lost Nation grew up not knowing who they were as Métis people—or if they did know, they didn't celebrate it. The Lost Generation had no sense of self.

The Found Nation is our new generation. My generation. The generation that is reclaiming their Métis identity and all that has been lost. The generation that is breaking away from shame and doing the work of reconnecting and learning our ways of knowing. It is incredibly beautiful to know the strength that comes with your identity. But I would not be telling the truth if I did not also mention how painful it can be to carry the weight of breaking through the shame and loss to enter a place of pride and connection. It took my people seven generations to find ourselves again. Each generation's experience is woven into the DNA of our young ones. Now that we are found, we will never be forgotten, we are sure of that.

In Michif, the word for "rising" is *waanishkow*; the command is *waanishka*. It quite literally means "get up and rise." Imagine your Kokum trying to wake you up in the morning and shouting "waanishka!" from the kitchen. I think this is the perfect word to describe Indigenous young people. We have not forgotten the genocide our families, communities and Nations have experienced, and continue to experience. We will never forget, as it is woven into our entire being. But genocide doesn't define us anymore: we are unapologetically and fearlessly rising. A revolution is brewing among us; it is a pivotal moment.

This is not to undermine or take away from all that those before us have done, all of the times they stood up and fought for justice—the Oka Crisis, the Battle of Batoche and the Treaty of 1752, for example. It is not to undermine the hard work of our people, such as Maria Campbell, Christine Welsh or Alanis Obomsawin, and every single time our people have stood up with courage and humility and looked oppression in the face, demanding our inherent rights. Louis Riel once said, "My people will sleep for 100 years, but when they awake, it will be the artists who give them their spirit back." Our existence, our resistance, our pride and our strength are an art. We have awoken. Step by step, young ones are taking their spirit back. It will be the privilege of my life to grow with these ones while we beautifully take back our rightful places and continue to pave the way for a future that is inherently Indigenous.

Recently, I was spending time in a circle of Elders, and one Kokum shared something that I have not stopped thinking about. She was explaining how important it is to be in circles like the one we were in and how foundational it is for our people to have young ones and old ones spending time together. She explained that as our old ones grow older their lights begin to dim, and as our young ones grow their lights grow brighter. She explained that there is a transmission of knowledge, the stories and teachings of our ancestors being passed on, as our old ones' lights begin to dim and our young ones' grow brighter. How grounding to know that our future is armed with young ones whose light is lit by our Ancestors, our history, our teachings and our people. It gives me chills. My Kokum always reminds me of the importance of reclaiming my power, my space, and to remember that I will never walk alone; Creator and my Ancestors are always with me. The only way I know how to describe it is "home." My light is armed with ancestral resilience, knowledge, wisdom and love—that, to me, feels like home.

I was gifted in ceremony with the responsibility of taking care of my people. This will be a responsibility I carry with me and take seriously for as long as I am on this earth. As an old one, part of my responsibility will be sharing knowledge and preparing our younger ones to take on new roles and responsibilities as our older generations begin their journeys to the spiritual world. Spending time with Elders and old ones has been foundational to my identity. There is not one thing more valuable to me than time spent with our Elders and hearing their stories and lived experiences. Having the opportunity to sit with Elders, share tea and listen to all they have to offer is one of the most culturally grounding opportunities I have been given. I dream of a generation of children who can grow up knowing their culture and identity, never having to know the shame or hurt our parents, grandparents, Elders and Ancestors once felt. I hope that when I am an old one, I will sit alongside our young ones and remind them how capable they are and how important each of their gifts is.

Our kinship systems are different from those in Western ways of knowing. I have siblings but I also take non-related people as my cousins, aunties and uncles. I have someone in my life who I take as my sister—my Eagle sister. We live six hundred kilometres apart, but our spirits are so connected that it gives me chills. We see eagles at the exact same time and share the same dreams, even while being so far apart, in different provinces. In the Seven Sacred Teachings, the Eagle is the teaching of love. My Elders taught me that to know love is to know peace. Love is at the centre of the medicine wheel, and it is symbolic of fire and Creator. Eagles are incredibly sacred to us: they fly the highest and closest to Creator. The sacred colours we were gifted by Elders blend at sunset, when my Eagle sister and I meet at the sky, closest to Creator, just like our sacred Eagle. We frequently have conversations about what it is like being a young Indigenous person leading in a movement. I called her recently, frustrated after a conversation I'd had with someone who questioned my identity and what culture meant to me, and who had a checklist in their mind to evaluate whether I met their idea of "spiritual." I called my Eagle sister, frustrated and disappointed that our own people questioned young ones this way and felt comfortable degrading us and making us feel "less than." I called her, bitter because this sickness based in colonial perspectives still exists within our people and communities. As always, she was calm, and our conversation motivated us to work harder, do better and reach deeper. There is no checklist for Indigeneity, and it is incredibly disappointing that we still have gatekeepers to our culture as we try and break the barriers. My eagle sister reminded me that our culture is peoplehood, a breathtaking thing.

Indigenous people are incredibly resilient, though we should never have had to be. There is a mayshchitew (home fire) that burns within us. I do not want to portray the revolution brewing among Indigenous young ones as easy, or as all "butterflies and rainbows." It is beautiful; there is no denying that. However, it must be acknowledged that there is immense struggle and challenge that comes with being an Indigenous young person facing colonial institutions and demanding better. There is a constant need to prove and defend our existence. It is devastating to already be living through the crises of suicide, substance abuse and environmental destruction, all while still having our identities questioned, like our Indigeneity needs to be proven. It is blood-boiling and humiliating that our very best are still being questioned. We face backlash from settlers who want to see the proof; the heat and lateral violence we sometimes take from our own people, as ugly as that is it to admit; and the ignorance of government and colonial institutions we have grown up seeing. We seek to tear down and rebuild the very institutions that tried to destroy us, and somehow we continue to look genocide in the face and rise above it all with guts, grit and humility. With every reason to be angry, we remain humble and love Mother Earth harder. It rings true that our love for our people is stronger than anyone's hate; there is no room for shame in our bundle.

Identity has been influential, if not everything, in my personal healing journey. Thinking back to my best moments, and even where I find myself now, I am centred in my identity and grounded in my culture. I can't speak for everyone, but I can say that the more time I spend with youth, with Elders and my community, the more I come to understand how influential identity is to our well-being. I see it with the youth I work with, as they come to learn about medicines and traditions, spend time with Elders and take part in ceremonies. I have the privilege of witnessing their spirits emerging, step by step. You see it in the way they walk, in the joy and love they have for others, and in the celebrations of their healing and new journeys. When they are connected with identity, it's like seeing the piece that was always missing find its place at home again. You get to witness the best versions of themselves blossoming, and it fills me with hope. We are breaking barriers in every single way, within our own ways and within Western ways of knowing. Our young ones are learning the language; some have even mastered it. Our young ones are learning the land and our traditional practices. Some of our young ones are pipe carriers, traditional hunters and gatherers, and master beaders. We are heart surgeons, lawyers, engineers, business owners, professors, teachers and community members. Indigenous student centres in post-secondary institutions across the country are filled with Indigenous people expanding their knowledge and dismantling the colonial goal that we would never enter these institutions. We are grounded in knowledge, and each role we occupy is foundational to our communities and our rise. The bar was set so low that it would be unwise to set an expectation for "success." We have broken through, shattered and risen above every standard they set; we are not the lazy, drunken, no-good Indians that colonialism loved to make us out to be.

Our ancestors paved the way so that we could build our dreams. For this we say Maarsii; their sacrifice is our existence. We are unapologetic Indigenous youth living our truth. We are the outcome of genocide survival; we have seven generations of strength woven into our existence. We not only rise as a whole, but we rise at every occasion in which we are let down and failed. We hold ourselves accountable to rising—Every. Single. Time. They say our medicine is love, but our young ones are the medicine. The future is inherently Indigenous, and it will be the privilege of my life to live every single day grounded in my culture and surrounded by this movement. I am filled with such hope every time I see our young ones get up and rise, and it is incredibly humbling to be among them. My hope is that if these pages come across the paths of our Chapans, Kokums and Mushums, they can find comfort in knowing that our youth are grounded in ancestral wisdom and will rise to the task of carrying our collective future forward, because they showed us the way. Their light lives within each of us. My hope is that if these pages are read by our parents, they will be reassured that they did the absolute best they could with what they had, and we are immensely grateful. I hope our matriarchs know that they raised warriors. Lastly, my hope is that if these pages find their way to our young ones, they can see themselves in the words and know that they have a place among us. We will meet you where you are at, share our love and welcome you home to the circle. You always have a place here, and we look forward to supporting your rise.

Welcome to our rise.

# We Appear to Have
# Fallen on Dark Times

**LEE MARACLE**
Writer & Traditional Teacher

GIVEN THE 2020 AMERICAN ELECTIONS AND THE ATTACK on the White House in early 2021, which was the response of the Right to a Democratic victory in the Senate, Congress and the presidency, it seems stability may not be the order of the day these days. To paraphrase Frantz Fanon—who said in *Wretched of the Earth* that just as soon as the darkest times are upon you, a new movement arises to pull you out of your oppression—it seems America is falling into the darkest of times. I mention this because so much of what happens in America affects what happens in Canada. And, of course, we are responsive to what happens in Canada. We appear to have fallen on our dark times. There have been dire warnings about the extinction of Indigenous language and culture for some time now, at least since I was a teenager. I know we are in the midst of a cultural revival among Salish people, which began with my bringing back some of our ceremonies in the late 1970s and '80s. This led to the revival of song and then language. What does that mean for the next hundred years? First, for the past hundred years we have endured illiteracy and a great lack of oracy. We have been remedying both of those things in equal measure in the past thirty years, with great vigour. One hundred years from now, our languages will be spoken not just by Indigenous people but by Europeans as well, if universities and schools have their way, as our languages are open to anyone to study. It will be difficult for us to accept this level of sharing, but in the end the culture requires it of us, and so we will. We will become the sharing people we once were.

WE ARE ALSO struggling with our illiteracy and becoming literate. University of Toronto President David Naylor once said in a speech to the recipient of the President's Indigenous Award that when Indigenous people graduate from high school on time, they attend university in greater numbers than any other race of people in Canada. The problem is that they do not graduate on time. We have been struggling with this ever since, and more and more of our youth are beginning to graduate from high school on time. If this trend continues, we will be the best educated poor people in Canada because what is not changing is the poverty line and us living below it. Many of our current Elders hold bachelor's and master's degrees and PhDs, which is inspiring our youth to stay in school. At the same time, few of those who are educated have places within the universities that educated them. One hundred years from now, most Indigenous people will be better educated than Canadians, but not necessarily better off.

WE HAVE A teaching that "everything begins with song." When I was studying sociology at university, an instructor said that Karl Marx said language came with the invention of tools. I laughed. The instructor asked me what was amusing. Before tools, humans ran down deer and rabbits, and they hand-caught fish. Before tools, mothers sang to their children and uttered sounds that they could negotiate with. These practices still go on in the world. No tools were required for communication or language to begin. What was required was a baby and a mother. From birth, mothers sing to their newborns, as do aunts, uncles and so on, even if it is just to hum vocables. The first human, "Lucy," was here two million years ago. She was Indigenous African. We do not know how she managed to survive and thrive, but she did. I have just returned from South Africa, where an Elder lamented, "Surely, there must be something valuable about our culture. We have been here for more than 350,000 years." It changed the direction of the discussion. This is the pebble that falls into the quiet pond and sends ripples out. More and more, we are connecting with other Indigenous people. If this continues, in a hundred years we will have huge influence on the social direction the world takes. Word Power through uniting Indigenous people is on the horizon.

It has been decades since I lay across my great-uncle Henry George's shoulder while he and my grandfather carved canoes and every now and then told stories. I often awoke to the stories. One that I particularly remember was about the Ancestors coming to sing and dance for me. The waters of Tsleil-Waututh (our name for Burrard Inlet, I was told) were alive on this one occasion. Tiny ripples dancing in the sunlight. I asked him what the ripples were, and he told a story about how the ancestors catch the attention of a child while watching over us and begin to dance. He said that if I listened carefully, I could hear them sing. I listened and soon he and Pappy were singing and looking out on the water. I could hear it. More importantly, it connected deeply with my emotionality. I am still moved by the song of earth and water. I followed the Elders around after that, waiting for the inevitable story. My children were raised with these stories as well. My daughter, Columpa Bobb, turned our bat story into a play. My son, Sid Bobb, and his wife formed Aanmitaagzi, and they mounted a community theatre play with the cedar of the stories. If this trend continues, our stories will be dramatized on Canadian stages.

We discussed things then. Problems, tensions, quarrels were talked about—not debated. Everyone participated, as though fishing for some earlier historical response to the same tension, quarrel or problem. Everyone listened for a solution, and no one got jealous because their solution was not picked. "This is how we are, Siem," would always end the discussion. This is rarely done these days, but we can pick this practice up again. At school with Europeans, I noticed that the discussion was an argument that ended when someone "won." While it was going on, the argument heated up and sometimes a fight broke out. I recall that the voices of quarrel hurt my collar bone, and I decided to go back to my teachings and retrieve myself from among the memories of my Elders. Others have joined me. If this keeps up, our cultures in one hundred years will be fully restored.

This is a long process, as the Elders that tell these stories are forever aging, but more and more, our young people are learning them. I imagine some young people have difficulty trusting memory; I know for a long time I did, but eventually I knew that I was as entitled to my memory of story as any of the Elders who originally told these stories. I determined to run with my memories. I began holding feasts and ceremonies, including my children in the process of storytelling and raising them from story, rather than from the principle of obedience. More and more young people are doing just that—picking up the ceremonies; trusting their hearts, their love and their spirits; and bringing culture. If this keeps up, in a hundred years we will have defeated all the lateral violence and meanness in our communities.

We will raise our children from song, story and dance, and nurture them with gratitude. Most of my relatives my age went to residential school—not all of them, but most. I did not have a consciousness as a young person that I was raised differently, but after joining the Red Power movement, I met several people who were also raised on story and we began patching ourselves together. I grew up in Salish territory, raised by grammas and grandpas who constantly reminded me that this is "Indian land"—we are in our original territory. We have been here since time immemorial and our first love is the land.

What will that mean a hundred years from now, Drew Taylor wants to know? Where will we be? I am going to answer this as though he is talking about our internal state of being and the direction we are moving in. Thousands of us now are attending public schools and graduating and going on to university. But we are doing so as Indigenous people wanting to reclaim our cultures, our ceremonies, our songs, our dances, and to move forward as who we are and will always want to be: Indigenous people.

History is always uneven and slightly off balance, so predictions are unreliable, but I was looking at a demonstration led by my relatives on the West Coast who are struggling to stop Kinder Morgan in order to save the salmon. My aunt, our Ta'ah, asked the men to "Warrior Up" almost two decades ago and they did. They began allying with Indigenous people and, as my nephew Rueben George said, "We are not just doing this for us, it is for you too." And by "you" he meant non-Indigenous people. We are inclusive. There is no word for "exclude" in our language. So he is building relationship between Salish people and the newcomers. That concept of allyship exists in America too, and it culminated in the defeat of Donald Trump, whose supporters could not accept the election results. If the conflict in the United States continues, it will heat up and people of colour and Indigenous people will find themselves in the sights of the rising domestic terrorist movement. In a hundred years, someone will likely have won the conflict, but it will not resolve the tension. We will not give in or give up. Not this year, next year or in a hundred years.

Violence is a sacred act. Humans must kill for their meals: whether it is vegetation or living flesh, something must die that we might live. And so we respect, honour and seek permission to participate in the procurement of food. Our violence becomes sacred through the ceremony and the good words before we kill. The taking of food was a promise we inherited from creation. Sing, say the good words, express our gratitude, treat all life as sacred and all will be well. Killing to solve a quarrel is just not the way to go, so if this tension heats up, we will just be in terrible trouble. I believe we will find a peaceful way to solve problems in the next hundred years.

Our belief is that we came here from the spirit world, to experience physicality so we can understand the sacred.

When we die, we return to the spirit world. This is for us the first sacred act of creation and recycling practised. I still believe this. I do not fear death. I feel for my relations who will miss me. I feel for myself, who will miss my relatives, but I do not fear death, because I can return. In fact, if we come across a Salish person who is exceptionally intelligent, we say, "They have been here before." My children were recognized as very old souls as small children, and they have not lost their perspective. They still phone to talk about story, what it means today and what they should be doing.

I have no criticism for anyone who picks up European values, religion, songs or dances. We have influenced all those things. Democracy is new to them. It originates from the cultural clash between us and them more than two hundred years ago. President Bill Clinton himself expressed gratitude for the Haudenausaunee constitution, borrowed as the foundation for democracy in centuries past. They also ought to thank us for such gifts as sanitation, environmental wellness and now well-being itself. I believe that we will continue the movement to become well. We have awakened. The Dene that Raymond Yakeleya speaks of have held several gatherings to reclaim themselves and heal from colonial oppression without killing the colonizer. We have a long way to go, but we can get there in a hundred years. I believe we want to be well.

The anti-colonial movements of the last century did not lead to our humanity. They were wars. The conflict heated up and people killed each other. It is just not the way to go. We are not entitled to life without consequence. That is, we are entitled to live, to kill to eat and to honour what food has died for us, but we are not entitled to kill because we do not like someone else's way of life. The Squamish Princess of Peace, Mary Agnes, believed that and so I inherit not just her blood line but her belief. I share that belief with every breath I take. I have come together with many people and we are building a new world as I speak. We are allying ourselves with other Indigenous people globally. We are allying ourselves with people of colour and white settlers who want to experience the good life in this country. We are building allegiances, relationships and new sensibilities across national, racial and colour lines. If we do this with vigour, we will turn the tide and change the way we do business here on this island. We will create a new world. In one hundred years this country will be embarking on a journey to wellness.

If we fail, we will return to the spirit and regroup. This is not the first time we have faced a terrible conflagration. It is not the first time the world has been threatened and the people in it died. We tried very hard to learn from the last great flood, which took the lives of most of the people of the world, but if we failed in passing on what we know to be true, what we remember in our bones, then we will just have to begin again. A hundred years from now, we will have triumphed or failed.

In any case, we will be back, to begin again, stauncher, braver and more loving than we have ever been. What is clear to me is that we have a sacred duty to connect with our past, to reconstruct our world, to rediscover our stories, our oldest oratory, so that we may begin again. If we do not have this knowledge in our living memory, we must find it in the memories of our dead.

We have entered the arts in unprecedented numbers, and we have brought our good words to the arts. From the mid-twentieth century, when the Indian agent forbade a young artist from attending art school, to today, thousands of us have picked up our creativity and our tobacco and have stumbled onto the world stage. We are a formidable and influential force. We always have been a formidable and influential force. We survived untold oppression from the dehumanized population that arrived here, and we humanized them. The world is different because we made it so. Some say we were romanticized, that our environmentalism was a fiction. I respond, the biggest trees in the world in 1886 lived in my back yard at Snauq'w (False Creek). It is common sense that killing things willfully is dangerous. Killing trees for paper that has no other purpose than wiping our backsides and advertising products for which we have no need is clearly psychotic.

Fifty years ago, a young Indigenous man told me that he hated people from India and Pakistan. "Whatever for?" I asked, without judgment. I was curious, and he answered, gritting his teeth, "They do not use toilet paper"—to which I replied, "What do you think your grandmothers used before white people cut down our trees, destroying whole forests, so we could have toilet paper?" Then I continued, "The irony is that even after using toilet paper, we still have to wash our hands." I laughed, "The people you purport to hate just skip the destroying-the-trees step. Truly, which is better?" Given global warming and deforestation, the death of whole species, I think we all know the answer. The question is, will we be brave enough and stalwart enough to do what we must do over the next hundred years?

Chaos is growing below the 49th parallel. The United States is a death machine—killing is what it does best. Patriarchy, racism, colonialism and gendered annihilation mark it. Killing lustfully, wantonly and wastefully is its everyday practice. It is what made Americans great in their own eyes. Thank god they are deeply divided. We have a chance to Warrior Up and turn the tide, not just for the animals, or the earth, or ourselves, but for our humanity. As Fanon said, and I paraphrase, If this fight is not for humanity, then it is not worth engaging in.

We have a story. When the tides receded, the men went to war. Men cannot be afraid, our Elders say; they must get angry when fear starts to rise. They must find a culprit to blame, to work out their anger. And that is usually other people. The women and children hid in the bush. The men went to war. A group of them killed women and children. Raven came to women and said, "These men have killed creation. They must do the dance of death." The women agreed and told the men what Raven had said. The men agreed to throw themselves on a great funeral pyre if the women would carry their bones and purify them for the next life. The women agreed. We will have to turn back the tide or do the dance of death.

I am throwing in my lot with us "doing the right thing," as Spike Lee says. One hundred years from now we will be more united on this island than ever before. We will have brought the knowledge of the world and begun the arduous task of reconstructing this ruined island. Our young people will lead the way, back toward our beliefs and forward toward their humanity. It will be a great time to be alive, and I will be looking down at my grandson's and granddaughters' aging children, who are such golden-hearted human beings, and I will swell with pride. I will have witnessed the second reclamation of earth and our humanity.

# About the Contributors

CYNDY BASKIN, PhD, is of Mi'kmaq and Celtic descent. Her clan is the Fish and her spirit name translates as something like The Woman Who Passes on the Teachings. She is an associate professor in the School of Social Work at Ryerson University in Toronto, a prolific writer and a training consultant in areas such as anti-violence work, homelessness, mental health and culture-based programming with Indigenous Peoples. Originally from New Brunswick, she lives in Toronto, Ontario.

MINADOO MAKWA BASKIN (Spirit-Bear) is Ojibwe and Mi'kmaq, of Bear clan teachings from Beausoleil First Nation. He studies public administration and governance at Ryerson University through the First Nations Technical Institute program. Currently he works at the Toronto Inuit Association as a Makitatsiatuq program coordinator, bringing fitness and health-based programing to Torontomiut (Toronto-Inuit). Makwa lives in Toronto, Ontario.

DR. NORMA DUNNING is an Edmonton-based Inuk writer, professor and grandmother. Her previous short story collection, *Annie Muktuk and Other Stories* (University of Alberta Press, 2017), received the Danuta Gleed Literary Award, the Howard O'Hagan Award for short stories and the Bronze Foreword INDIES award.

Her first poetry collection, *Eskimo Pie: A Poetics of Inuit Identity* (BookLand), was published in 2020, and her second collection of short stories, *Tainna (the unseen ones)* (Douglas & McIntyre), was released in 2021.

SHELLEY KNOTT FIFE, an Anishnaabekwe, resides where she was raised, in her home community of Curve Lake First Nation. She has worked in First Nations education for over twenty years— as education manager for Curve Lake First Nation, a provincial school board consultant, an Indigenous education officer for the Ontario Ministry of Education, and currently as an education specialist with Indigenous Services Canada. She is a PhD candidate in Indigenous Studies at Trent University, focusing her research on special education and Indigenous students.

JORDANNA GEORGE is an artist from the T'Sou-ke Nation, raised in Sooke, British Columbia, now living in the Vancouver area on Tsleil-Waututh territory. Having studied visual art at the University of Victoria, they now create illustrations and comics, often centring LGBT+ identities and taking inspiration from their culture, genre fiction and human emotion. You can find them at jordannageorge.com.

SHALAN JOUDRY is a Mi'kmaw poet, playwright, oral storyteller and ecologist. Using her theatrical background, shalan brings Mi'kmaw stories to a new generation of listeners, as well as recounting personally crafted narratives that follow Mi'kmaw storying custom. shalan is the author of two books of poetry, *Generations Re-merging* (Gaspereau Press, 2014) and *Waking Ground* (Gaspereau Press, 2020), and the play *Elapultiek* (Pottersfield Press, 2019), inspired by real-life species at risk. She lives with her family in their community of L'sətkuk (Bear River First Nation), in shalan's home territory of Kespukwitk, in southwest Nova Scotia.

TAE:HOWĘHS, AKA AMOS KEY JR. is a member of the Mohawk Nation. He is an educator and advocate who has worked as a secondary school teacher in London, Ontario; director of First Nations languages at the Woodland Cultural Centre in Brantford, Ontario, for thirty-five years; assistant professor at the University of Toronto's Centre for Indigenous Studies; and Indigenous vice-provost at Brock University. Amos is currently the executive director of CKRZ 100.3 FM, and is consulting with the First Nations Technical Institute at Tyendinega Mohawk Nation on the establishment of Ontario's inaugural Bachelor of Indigenous Education for Second Language and Immersion Instructors.

TRACIE LÉOST is an award-winning young Métis leader, activist and athlete from St. Laurent, Manitoba, in Treaty 1 territory. Her strong commitment to contributing to social justice is evidenced by the philanthropic and awareness initiatives she has spearheaded. In 2020, she founded Waanishka Movement Inc., a non-profit organization that supports Indigenous youth to rise. Tracie upholds her responsibilities as an emerging matriarch by serving her people and ensuring that all Indigenous youth have opportunities to grow and flourish.

CLARENCE LOUIE has been Chief of the Osoyoos Indian Band for eighteen terms. He has received the Aboriginal Business Leader Award from All Nations Trust and Development Corporation and has been chairperson of the Aboriginal Business Canada Board. Moreover, Clarence was the first Native ever inducted into the Canadian Business Hall of Fame in 2018. He has negotiated many multimillion-dollar land claim settlements on behalf of his band, and he is a member of both the Order of British Columbia and the Order of Canada. He lives in Osoyoos, British Columbia.

LEE MARACLE, a member of the Stó:lō Nation, is an award-winning author, a Traditional Teacher and an instructor at the University of Toronto's Centre for Indigenous Studies. She has written countless works, including novels and collections of poetry, short stories and essays. A recipient of the Queen's Diamond Jubilee medal, she was also appointed as an Officer of the Order of Canada in 2018 for her many contributions to Canada's literary landscape. She lives in Toronto, Ontario.

DARREL J. MCLEOD is Nehiyaw (Cree) from Northern Canada, Treaty 8. He has been a French immersion teacher, school principal in Yekooche First Nation, director of a curriculum centre, executive director of Education and International Affairs at the Assembly of First Nations, and chief negotiator for the Government of Canada. He is fluent in French, Spanish and English, and is studying Cree. Darrel's memoir, *Mamaskatch: A Cree Coming of Age* (Douglas & McIntyre), won the 2018 Governor General's Literary Award for non-fiction, was shortlisted for several other prestigious awards, and has been published in French and German. Its sequel, *Peyakow: Reclaiming Cree Dignity* (Douglas & McIntyre), was published in 2021. Darrel is now finishing his first novel. He lives near Sooke, British Columbia, and winters in Puerto Vallarta, Mexico, reading, writing, and singing jazz songs.

AUTUMN PELTIER is from Wikwemikong First Nation/Manitoulin Island and is of Ojibway/Odawa heritage. She is the Anishinabek Nation chief water commissioner. A world-renowned water-rights advocate and leading global environmental activist, she has spoken about contaminated water on Indigenous reserves in Canada at the United Nations General Assembly. For her work and activism, Peltier was nominated for the International Children's Peace Prize in 2017, 2018 and 2019. She lives in Ottawa, Ontario.

ROMEO SAGANASH, born on the land, is a Cree jurist from the boreal forest near his community of Waswanipi, Québec. He served as a Member of Parliament from 2011 to 2019. He is the founder of the Cree Nation Youth Council, and spent more than two decades debating, drafting and negotiating the United Nations

Declaration on the Rights of Indigenous Peoples (UNDRIP). He intended to move to British Columbia after his political career; he made it halfway, and now lives in Winnipeg, Manitoba.

DREW HAYDEN TAYLOR is an award-winning playwright, novelist, scriptwriter and journalist. He was born and raised on the Curve Lake First Nation in Central Ontario. Taylor has authored over thirty books, including *Chasing Painted Horses* (Cormorant Press, 2019) which won the 2020 PMC Indigenous Literature Award. He also edited *Me Funny, Me Sexy* and *Me Artsy* (Douglas & McIntyre, 2006, 2008 and 2015), and has been nominated for two Governor General's Awards. He lives on the Curve Lake First Nation in Ontario.

RAYMOND YAKELEYA is an award-winning Sahtú Dene filmmaker, producer, director and writer with over thirty years of experience in the television industry. He has studied photography and electronic media at the Banff Centre for Arts and Creativity and filmmaking at the University of Southern California in Los Angeles. He has produced five national television series and his documentary films have been shown at festivals and museums around the world, including the Museum of the American Indian in New York and the British Museum of Mankind in London. Originally from Tulita, Northwest Territories, Raymond now lives in Edmonton, Alberta.

COMPILED *and* EDITED *by*

*Drew* HAYDEN TAYLOR

{ not pictured here }

# ME FUNNY

A *far-reaching* exploration of the HUMOUR, wittiness and repartee DOMINANT among the *First Nations people* of North America, as witnessed, *experienced* and CREATED DIRECTLY by themselves, and with the INCLUSION of outside *but reputable* sources necessarily *familiar* with the INDIGENOUS sense of humour as SEEN from an *objective perspective*

# Me Funny (2005)

HUMOUR HAS ALWAYS been an essential part of North American Indigenous culture. This fact remained unnoticed by most settlers, however, since non-Indigenous people just didn't get the joke. Indians, it was believed, never laughed. But Indians themselves always knew better.

As an award-winning playwright, columnist and comedy-sketch creator, Drew Hayden Taylor has spent fifteen years writing and researching Indigenous humour. For this book, he asked a leading group of writers from a variety of fields—among them such celebrated wordsmiths as Thomas King, Lee Maracle and Tomson Highway—to take a look at what makes Indigenous humour tick. Their challenging, informative and hilarious contributions examine the use of humour in areas as diverse as stand-up comedy, fiction, visual art, drama, performance, poetry, traditional storytelling and education. As *Me Funny* makes clear, there is no single definition of Indigenous humour. But the contributors do agree on some common ground: Native humour pushes the envelope. With this collection, readers will have the unforgettable opportunity to appreciate that for themselves.

ISBN: 978-1-55365-137-6
E-BOOK ISBN: 978-1-92668-572-4

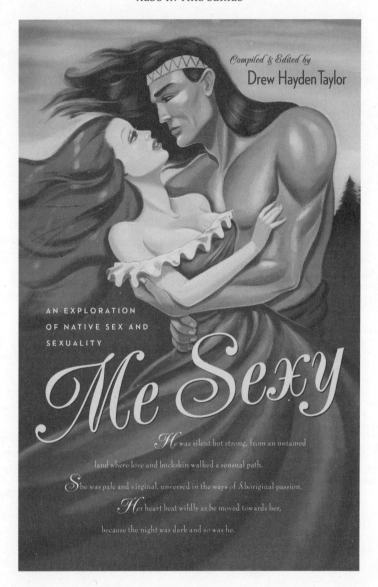

Compiled & Edited by
Drew Hayden Taylor

AN EXPLORATION
OF NATIVE SEX AND
SEXUALITY

*Me Sexy*

*He was silent but strong, from an untamed*

*land where love and buckskin walked a sensual path.*

*She was pale and virginal, unversed in the ways of Aboriginal passion.*

*Her heart beat wildly as he moved towards her,*

*because the night was dark and so was he.*

# Me Sexy (2012)

THIS MOVING AND often funny look at Native sexuality from some of Canada's best First Nations and Inuit writers is the sequel to the highly successful *Me Funny*. *Me Sexy* is an anthology containing thirteen contributions from leading members of North America's First Nations writing communities. The many highlights include Lee Maracle's creation story, Salish style; Tomson Highway explaining why Cree is the sexiest of all languages; Marius P. Tungilik looking at the dark side of Inuit sex; and Marissa Crazytrain discussing her year as a stripper in Toronto, and how it shaped her life back in Saskatchewan. A smart and creative collection, *Me Sexy* will thrill all kinds of readers.

ISBN: 978-1-92668-573-1

E-BOOK ISBN: 978-1-92668-573-1

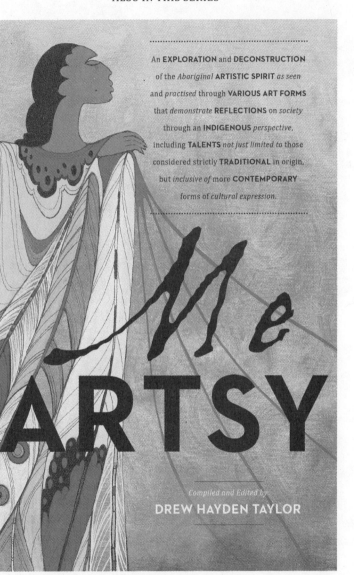

An **EXPLORATION** and **DECONSTRUCTION** of the *Aboriginal* **ARTISTIC SPIRIT** *as seen* and *practised* through **VARIOUS ART FORMS** that *demonstrate* **REFLECTIONS** on *society* through an **INDIGENOUS** *perspective*, including **TALENTS** *not just limited to* those considered strictly **TRADITIONAL** in origin, but *inclusive of* more **CONTEMPORARY** forms of *cultural expression*.

*Me*

# ARTSY

*Compiled and Edited by*
**DREW HAYDEN TAYLOR**

# Me Artsy (2015) ·

WHILE FIRST NATIONS cultural practice still honours traditional forms, contemporary Indigenous artists have diversified into many areas. The fourteen contributors whose essays make up *Me Artsy* pursue such varied disciplines as filmmaking, gourmet cuisine, blues piano, fashion design, acting, writing and painting as well as traditional drumming and storytelling. Their concerns include the eternal ones that occupy artists everywhere—how does one get started, where do you find inspiration, how does one make a living. What makes *Me Artsy* special is that all these concerns are always overlaid with an awareness of First Nations identity.

Chef David Wolfman describes gruelling years in the kitchens of the exclusive National Club; filmmaker Zacharias Kunuk discusses leaping into his first feature film without knowing how to finance it; and playwright Drew Hayden Taylor tells the story of putting a bullet through his first play and burying it in his yard. Other contributors include actor/playwright Monique Mojica, painter Marianne Nicolson, fashion designer Kim Picard, painter Maxine Noel, blues pianist Murray Porter, scholar Karyn Recollet, dancer/choreographer Santee Smith, director/actor Rose Stella, traditional drummer Steve Teekens, writer and storyteller Richard Van Camp and manga artist Michael Nicoll Yahgulanaas.

ISBN: 978-1-77162-070-3
E-BOOK ISBN: 978-1-77162-071-0